Creating learning without limits

*Mandy Swann, Alison Peacock, Susan Hart,
Mary Jane Drummond*

Open University Press

Open University Press
McGraw-Hill Education
McGraw-Hill House
Shoppenhangers Road
Maidenhead
Berkshire
England
SL6 2QL

email: enquiries@openup.co.uk
world wide web: www.openup.co.uk

and Two Penn Plaza, New York, NY 10121-2289, USA

First published 2012

A catalogue record of this book is available from the British Library

ISBN-13: 978-0-33-524211-5 (pb)
ISBN-10: 0-33-524211-1 (pb)
ebook: 978-0-33-524213-9

Library of Congress Cataloging-in-Publication Data
CIP data applied for

Typeset by RefineCatch Limited, Bungay, Suffolk
Printed in the UK by Ashford Colour Press Ltd

The *McGraw-Hill* Companies

This book is dedicated to our colleagues Donald McIntyre and Annabelle Dixon who were closely involved in the *Learning without Limits* project from its inception. Both have made irreplaceable contributions and are deeply missed.

"This will undoubtedly turn out to be amongst the most important educational books of the decade. Our capacity to respond, both individually and collectively, to its key insights and messages will profoundly affect not just the quality of our schools, but of our society for years to come.

Engagingly and eloquently written, it exposes the intellectual bankruptcy and human destructiveness of widely held concepts of 'ability' and offers a richly textured, practical account of how one school moved from 'failure' to OfSTED 'outstanding' by committing itself to the practicability of a morally inspiring, educationally convincing alternative.

If you want to know why 'the standards agenda' must inevitably fail and what we might do instead, read this book."

Professor Michael Fielding, Institute of Education,
University of London, UK

"This is an inspiring and reviving book. It reminds us why people come into education - to make a difference for children. To make a deep difference we have to organize education differently. It describes a school that vibrates with learning in an atmosphere of deep humanity and care. Its practices are light years away from the measuring, labelling, targeting, and testing structures that have become our recent national norm. The school as a whole community transforms people."

Anne Watson, Professor of Mathematics Education,
University of Oxford, UK

"This book provides a grounded demonstration of the importance of educational principles, the most important of which is the understanding that each child's potential for learning is limitless. The authors describe new school and classroom practices through which learning can be transformed. Their argument has influenced government thinking on the review of the National Curriculum in England. I urge you to let it influence your thinking too!"

Professor Andrew Pollard, Institute of Education,
University of London, UK

"This is a brilliant study of a small and very successful primary school in Hertfordshire where the teachers have rejected ideas of fixed innate ability and believe instead in the limitless potential of all young people. At a time when the Ofsted inspection process employs dubious and limited notions of 'standards' and 'achievement', it would be good to think that there could be many more schools like this one showing the way towards a new and liberating view of human development. The book deserves a really wide readership."

Professor Clyde Chitty, Institute of Education,
University of London, UK

Contents

Tables and figures

Tables

Figures

Preface

This is the story of a school – a primary school in Hertfordshire – which we have studied over a number of years. We, the research team and the headteacher, undertook the study in order to understand more about the big idea that was at the heart of the developments that took place there during the research period. As we shall show, in many respects The Wroxham School is not unlike thousands of other schools up and down the country. The building is typical of its type; the profile of learners is not unusual. The staff group has a predictable range of experience and qualifications. The budget is not enhanced in any way. The school is subject to the same pressures and demands from the local authority, Department for Education and the Office for Standards in Education as every other school.

But there is one feature of Wroxham that makes it distinctive: the vision that guides the work of the whole community, and the model of school development to which it gives rise. Embedded in that work is a fundamentally different view of learners and learning, of curriculum and pedagogy, from that promoted by the standards agenda, and a radically different approach to the distribution of leadership, power, monitoring and accountability.

Note on authorship

It is important to clarify who exactly 'we' refers to throughout this text. Alison Peacock, headteacher of The Wroxham School, has had a dual role as both a member of the research team and a member of the school staff. Being both an insider and an outsider to the research has created many challenges for Alison, not least in terms of writing up the Wroxham story. Although Alison has contributed fully to the development of the research and to the formulation of ideas for this book, she has found it uncomfortable, if not impossible, to write about herself and her work with colleagues in her own voice. We (all four co-authors) agreed that the best compromise would be to write the text from the 'outside' perspective of the university-based research team learning from the Wroxham staff. Therefore 'we' refers in most cases to the members of the university research team, though the text has been validated and revised in dialogue with Alison throughout the process of writing.

Acknowledgements

We would like to thank the staff, children, parents and governors of The Wroxham School for making this book possible by giving their time so generously. We are particularly grateful to Sophie Gilbert, Cheryl Mence, Simon Putman, Darrelle Todd, Jo Turner, Sarah Tustin and Martyn Vandewalle, and to Jenny Bramley and Samantha Revell who contributed to the first phase of the research.

We thank Non Worrall for her contribution to the work of data collection.

We are grateful to the Esmée Fairbairn Foundation and Hertfordshire local authority for providing funding for the research and to Martin Bailey for his support.

We were extremely privileged to have been supported by the invaluable insights, advice and guidance of Professor Donald McIntyre, who, as a member of the steering group, helped us to conceptualize and plan this enquiry and to formulate the research questions. He made significant contributions to the analysis and understanding of the data we were collecting, until his untimely death in 2007.

1   An alternative improvement agenda

Swimming against the tide: the premise for the research

We began this research drawn together by some unshakeable convictions: that human potential is not predictable, that children's futures are unknowable, that education has the power to enhance the lives of all. Few would argue with these simple truths, and yet they are at odds with the prevailing spirit of the age, a time in which teachers are required to use the certainty of prediction as a reliable tool in their planning and organization of opportunities for learning. Targets, levels, objectives, outcomes – all these ways of conceptualizing learning require teachers to behave as if children's potential is predictable and their futures knowable far in advance, as if their powers as educators can have only a limited impact on the lives of many children and young people. Furthermore, closely associated with this view of learning (as linear, measurable and quantifiable) is an equally damaging view of the children who do the learning, who can themselves be known, measured and quantified in terms of so-called ability, a fixed, internal capacity, which can readily be determined.

This determinist thinking is not limited to those of any particular political persuasion. Nor is it an issue of transient significance. It is the legacy of a long-standing and ongoing, deep-rooted orthodoxy about the nature of 'ability' and how best to set about educating children. This legacy has given rise to limited and limiting thinking on the part of policy makers about children and about how to structure and organize learning and schooling that is widely shared, as the following three extracts show.

Back in 2005, when our research project was just beginning, a recently published education White Paper, *Higher Standards, Better Schools for All*, drew on these damaging beliefs about differential ability and potential to express government commitment (in this example New Labour) to the maximum progress of every child: 'We must make sure that every pupil, gifted or talented, struggling or just average, reaches the limits of their capability' (DfES 2005: 1.28).

Let us pause, for a moment, to digest this single sentence. Its sentiment, though intended to be aspirational, is essentially deterministic, even fatalistic. It assumes that children naturally fall into one of these four categories and that it is right and proper to think of children in this way. It suggests that there are limits to every child's capability that can be known and reached, that to struggle is a sign of failure, and that to be 'just average' compared to those thought to be 'gifted or talented' is by definition to be second rate.

Five years on, and after a change of government, this determinist thinking continues to permeate the pronouncements of ministers. In 2010, for example, addressing a group of MPs, Michael Gove, the Education Secretary, was reported as saying:

> Children from wealthy backgrounds of low cognitive ability overtake children from poor backgrounds and high cognitive ability before they even arrive at school . . . So, in effect, rich thick kids do better than poor clever children, and when they arrive at school the situation as they go through gets worse.
>
> (Clark 2010)

While the concern to act on inequality of opportunity is surely welcome, if we unpack the conceptual apparatus used to formulate this concern, we can see that it perpetuates deeply limiting beliefs about ability and potential. It assumes not only that, as part of the natural order of things, there simply *are* 'clever' children and 'thick' children, but also that we can determine which are which from their differing attainments at a very early age. High and low ability are treated as fixed, stable states; those who are 'clever' have greater potential for learning than those of lower ability, so we must and should expect more of the former. These assumptions – about ability and potential – give rise to ill-placed confidence in the linearity and predictability of learning. Children are expected to progress in line with their presumed potential; only if they do not is there concern that something may be awry. So early differences in children's attainment – before they even arrive at school – take on a massive, predictive significance, setting expectations and influencing practices that shape the whole course of a child's future school career as a learner. Linearity and predictability are mainstays of the current 'reform' agenda. The emphasis of policy across parties is on children attaining at each stage of their schooling the differential targets that have been predicted from their attainments at previous stages. Learning, in this view, is a ladder up which children must climb (in broad groups) steadily, consistently, and in time together from rung to rung towards predetermined outcomes.

Since the publication of the 2005 White Paper, and in the name of raising standards, the drive to measure children's progress up the ladder has increasingly affected many aspects of teachers' and children's lives in school. The use of numerical 'levels' has become so ubiquitous that both descriptions of individual children and differences between children are now primarily formulated in terms of levels. At parents' evenings, parents find themselves hearing about their children's learning not in all its rich and multifaceted variety, but about their levels. Their child, they may be bewildered to be told, 'is a secure 3b in reading' but only 'a 2c in writing'. Teachers are encouraged to plan, predict, report on progress and express concerns specifically in terms of levels (whether children are reaching, failing to reach or exceeding 'expected' levels). Attaching a level to the performance of each child on a daily basis and, indeed, discussing with children what they need to do to move up to the next level, have become widely used practices. Special booster groups, with accompanying teaching materials, have been set up to help children to move up a level in the Standard Assessment Tasks (SATs), as have special courses for teachers in Key Stage 2 to help them lift the achievement of those at level 3 to a level 4 before taking their SATs. Children whose current levels are thought to be too far below those of their peers are routinely given different tasks to do 'at their level', often carried out with a teaching assistant outside the classroom. These dehumanizing ways of conceptualizing learners, learning, progress and achievements invite children and young people constantly to compare themselves with others, rather than fostering a strong positive sense of themselves as competent, complex, creative people each capable of playing a full part within a collaborative learning community. They prevent young people, and their teachers, from experiencing and savouring the joys and endless possibilities of learning. Permeating, as they do, the avalanche of policy and directives, they inevitably affect teachers' beliefs as well as their practices, especially those of beginning teachers.

There is another way

Yet the determinist views of learning and ability that underlie the ladder model are deeply flawed, as many decades of research have shown (Hart *et al.* 2004). Alexander (2001, 2008) has pointed out, following extensive comparative studies of primary education in many countries, that elsewhere in the world key terms in the educational lexicon tend to be more suggestive of cultural rather than natural influences and of external agency in learning. Teachers need a much more complex understanding of learning and of the many interacting influences that underlie differences of attainment if they are to be able to use their powers as educators to transform children's life chances. So, what if teachers were to jettison the linear model of learning at the heart of existing models of school improvement? What if, instead of being constantly compared, ranked, and fettered by labels, children's learning capacity was enabled to flourish and expand in all its rich variety and complexity? What if planning for preordained and predicted levels was replaced with planning experiences and opportunities for learning that promote deep engagement, that fill children with a sense of agency, that endow them with motivation, courage and belief in their power to influence their own futures? And what if school development were to be driven by a commitment on the part of a whole-school community to creating better ways for everybody to live, work and learn together, in an environment free from limiting beliefs about fixed abilities and fixed futures?

In this book we argue that school development inspired by this alternative vision is both necessary and possible. We present the findings of our research study of one primary school which, in just a few years, moved out of special measures to become a successful, vibrant learning community (also rated 'outstanding' by Ofsted), not through the use of targets, planning, prediction and externally imposed blueprints for pedagogy but through a focus on learning (rather than simply attainment), nourished by deep belief in the learning capacity of everybody. This alternative approach, as we shall show, is no easy option. It is highly demanding of all those involved. The crucial difference is that the demands are born of the challenges that staff set themselves arising from their firmly held principles and beliefs about learning rather than driven by external accountability. The purpose of this book is to explore how these dramatic changes were achieved and what lessons can be learnt from the experiences of this one school that can support other schools in developing their own approaches.

The original *Learning without Limits* project

Some of the principles which informed developments at Wroxham had their origins in a previous study at the Faculty of Education in Cambridge. This earlier study had explored alternatives to ability-based pedagogy, drawing on the thinking and practice of individual teachers working in a variety of different contexts. The *Learning without Limits* project (Hart *et al.* 2004) was designed to learn from and give a voice to teachers motivated by a particular view of learning: learning free from the unnecessary limits imposed by ability-based practices. The study was prompted by awareness that while decades of research had demonstrated the unintended damage that can be done – to children, teachers, and curriculum – by ability labelling and other practices derived from false assumptions about IQ and fixed ability (see Appendix A for a comprehensive evidence base), there was still no credible, articulated alternative to ability-based pedagogy. It was a matter of profound concern, the research team reasoned, that these assumptions not only continued to have currency in schools, but in recent years had been given new strength and legitimacy as part of government-sponsored initiatives to raise standards and improve practice in schools. They believed that studying the work of teachers who resolutely maintained an optimistic view of human educability would enable them to propose an alternative model and agenda for improvement, backed up by evidence.

The nine teachers who joined the research team of the original project worked with young people aged from 5 to 16 and had expertise in different curriculum areas. While their practices were distinctively individual, the research team found that they shared a radically different mindset, a different way of making sense of what happens in classrooms, based on a radically different orientation to the future that came to be called 'transformability'. Rather than accepting apparent differences in ability as the natural order of things, and differentiating their teaching accordingly, these teachers did not see the future of their students as predictable or inevitable. They worked on the assumption that there is always the potential for change: things can change for the better, sometimes even dramatically, as a result of what both teachers and learners do in the present.

For these teachers the concept of inherent ability, an inaccessible inner force responsible for learning, residing in the individual and subject to the fixed, internal limits of each individual learner, had no currency or value. In its place, the research team discerned the powerful alternative concept of learning capacity, which resides both in the individual learner and in the social collective of the classroom, and is by no means fixed and stable. This concept of learning capacity, evidenced in the various daily practices of these teachers, released the teachers from the sense of powerlessness induced by the idea of inherent ability. Furthermore, they realized that the work of transforming learning capacity does not depend on what teachers do alone, but on what both teachers *and* learners do – a joint enterprise, the exercise of co-agency. Convinced of their own (and their students') power to make a difference to future learning, they used their rich fund of knowledge about the forces – internal and external, individual and collective – that shape and limit learning capacity to make transforming choices. Working on the principle that classroom decisions must be made in the interests of all students, not just some – a principle the research team called 'the ethic of everybody' – and rooting their work in the fundamental trust in their students' powers as learners, the project teachers made good their commitment to the essential educability of their learners.

The study amassed convincing evidence that teaching for learning without limits is not a naïve fantasy, but a real possibility, in good working order, accessible to observation and analysis. The research team developed a practical, principled, pedagogical model (see Figure 1.1), arguing that elements of this model would be recognizable to other teachers who shared similar values and commitments and had themselves developed classroom practices in line with their convictions. They hoped that their work would convince more teachers that the alternative 'transformability' model is a practical and empowering way of realizing their commitment to young people's learning.

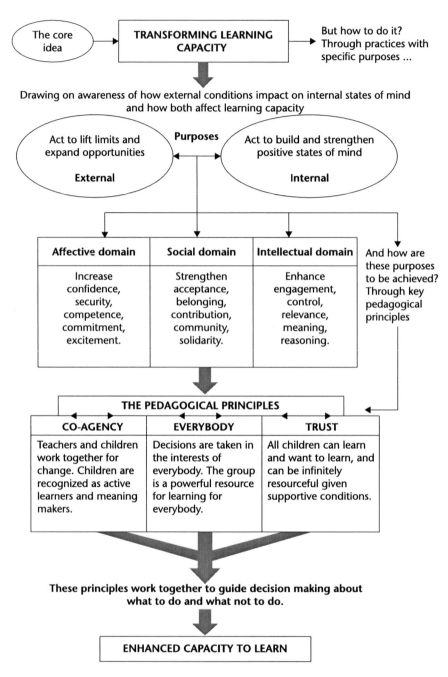

Figure 1.1 A practical, principled, pedagogical model

Source: Adapted from Hart *et al.* (2004).

However, the nine teachers in the original study were all working in different schools, in different parts of the country. The focus was inevitably limited to what teachers found themselves able to do individually, within their own classrooms, while subject to the same statutory curricular requirements, external expectations and national assessment pressures as every other teacher. These nine teachers all recognized that there was so much more that could be done to lift limits on learning and enhance the learning capacity of their students if groups of teachers, departments, whole-school staffs or even whole-school communities were to work together towards a common vision, with shared principles and purposes to guide their work of creating environments for learning free from the constraints imposed by ability labelling and ability-based practices.

The next step: *Creating Learning without Limits*

When one of the teachers who participated in the original project, Alison Peacock, took up a headship in a primary school that was designated by Ofsted as requiring 'special measures' (a failing inspection category), a wonderful opportunity presented itself to explore these wider possibilities. Alison was committed to leading staff in adopting teaching and learning practices devoted to strengthening and transforming children's learning capacity and free from all forms of ability labelling. A new research project was set up, *Creating Learning without Limits*, with funding from the Esmée Fairbairn Foundation and Hertfordshire local authority, to carry out a two-year in-depth study of the work of the staff of The Wroxham School in Hertfordshire. As our enquiry began we did not know what would be involved in developing and sustaining such an environment, but we hoped that through the study we would be able to build a convincing body of evidence to show that this alternative approach to school improvement could lead to the development of practices altogether more humane, equitable and life-enhancing for everybody.

This book tells the story of what we learned from the school community about how to create learning without limits. Our enquiry did not simply focus on individual teachers at the school or their teaching but also on the learning that does and must go on, individually and collectively, as the whole staff of a school work together, day by day, to create in reality their vision of an education based on inclusive, egalitarian principles, including an unshakeable bedrock belief in everybody's capacity to learn. In writing about this school we will show that it is possible to resist the pressures of performativity and the standards agenda, and for school development to be guided by such a vision. We chose to study The Wroxham School not because it is unique, or perfect, but because we know that this is a school where the staff group has become committed to and actively works towards this alternative vision; they show us both that it is possible and demonstrate how it is possible there, for them, on their terms – not the only way undoubtedly – but one successful way. By studying their ideas, interactions and practices we can learn more about what is involved, the dilemmas and struggles as well as the joys and successes, in making it a reality.

Being in the 'bottom set'

Alison Peacock first encountered The Wroxham School, a one form entry primary school with nursery in Potters Bar, Hertfordshire, in July 2002 as a prospective applicant for the post of headteacher. She found a school in trouble. The school had been judged by Ofsted in May 2001 to require special measures. One teacher recalls an Ofsted inspector describing a class as 'unteachable'. SATs results in the school had declined dramatically and remained stubbornly low. Her Majesty's Inspectorate (HMI) reported that there was massive underachievement throughout the school. The experience of being in special measures since 2001 had given the school an aura of desperation and weariness. Alison recalls that, post 2001, the response of senior management and other staff, in line with their perception of HMI expectations, had been to narrow the curriculum still further, with teaching time overwhelmingly dominated by English, mathematics and science, since these were tested each year at the ages of 7 and 11.

Nearly two years later, during an inspection in December 2002, HMI judged that only minimal progress had been achieved. HMIs had repeatedly observed, and Alison also saw on her arrival, that classroom behaviour for the most part was tightly controlled and suppressed, although there were also extreme incidents of furniture being thrown and children running off site. There was little evidence of engagement with learning or effort on the part of many children. Alison noticed that the Year 6 children were part of a youth culture that derisively labelled any peer who showed interest in learning as a 'boffin'. Many parents complained that their children were bored and unchallenged; some parents also expressed worries about bullying. Alison was not deterred, however, by what she found. On the contrary, she chose the school *because* of its circumstances. The experience of being placed in 'special measures' following an Ofsted inspection brought about similarly debilitating effects for the staff of a school, she thought, as the well-documented demoralization and loss of a sense of competence and capability that tend to follow from young people's placement in a 'bottom set'. She was inspired by the challenge of showing not only that it was possible to turn things around, but also that a different approach to school development could succeed where the 'blame and shame' model had failed. Reflecting on the reasons why she chose Wroxham, Alison recalled how 'I'd probably chosen to come to Wroxham because it was in the bottom set. I hadn't consciously recognized that's what I'd done . . . I wanted to prove there was another way of doing things.' Her confidence has been shown to be well justified. Since her appointment in January 2003, the school has been inspected by HMI three times, and four times by Ofsted. Following very rapid improvement in standards of behaviour, engagement, leadership, management systems, appearance, levels of motivation, parental satisfaction and feedback from the children, the school was taken out of special measures in October 2003 and was among the 100 top performing schools in 2004–5 based on the 'value added' measure of progress between Key Stages 1 and 2. It was recognized by Ofsted as 'outstanding' in 2006 and again in 2009.

Alison's approach to leadership

Alison's confidence that, with support and leadership based on *Learning without Limits* principles, dramatic changes could be made at Wroxham, derived in part from her previous experience as a teaching deputy head in a nearby school. There, as a class teacher, her practice had been predicated on her conviction that each individual child must – and could – be offered an irresistible invitation to join a shared learning journey. She worked to create a learning environment where it was safe to take risks, where confidence would increase, where everybody would become caught up in the excitement of learning. All children would be given the opportunity to develop the capacity to surprise themselves and those around them.

It was at this school that Alison had participated in the *Learning without Limits* research project. Alison's thinking and teaching feature as a case study in this publication, contributing to the development of the core idea of 'transformability' and the key purposes and principles that lie at the heart of teaching free from determinist beliefs about ability. As these ideas about pedagogy were being elaborated by the research team, Alison frequently asserted her belief that they applied just as much to adult learning as to children's learning, and that the model of classroom pedagogy could not be fully effective for children unless the same principles and purposes were also being applied to support the learning of the teaching team. The purposes and principles could, Alison suggested, form the basis of an alternative approach to school improvement.

In the pedagogical model presented in *Learning without Limits,* and shown here as Figure 1.1, teachers are conceptualized as working simultaneously on two different fronts – internal and external – to enable positive change to happen. Using their understanding of what can limit learning, both in the learning environment and within the minds of young people, teachers strive to enrich and enhance learning opportunities in ways that will also impact positively on young people's states of mind: their belief in themselves as learners, their attitudes to learning, their sense of belonging and their willingness to invest emotionally and intellectually in their learning in school. Alison believed that these same core purposes should apply to her work with staff. Everything she did from her first day needed to be directed towards building more positive states of mind among staff as well as children. She recalled, 'As headteacher, I saw my role as someone who should seek out even the tiniest chance to foster and nurture confidence amongst the staff so that they could begin to approach school differently.' Each member of the school community should be enabled to believe in themselves as learners for whom the next irresistible challenge was always within reach. In a school such as this no one, adult or child, would be 'written off', each person would be valued as an individual whose learning would never have a ceiling set upon it. Everyone within the school community needed to believe that the future was in the making in the present, and that their every action in the here and now could lead to a new way forward.

Alison believed that the three key pedagogical principles – co-agency, trust and everybody – in the *Learning without Limits* model also had direct, practical relevance for her approach to leadership. In the classroom context, the principle of *co-agency* focuses on the necessity for change to be achieved by teachers and children working together. The principle guides teachers towards decisions that they believe will increase children's active participation and control over their learning, their positive sense of themselves as competent thinkers and learners and their ability and willingness to engage in and commit themselves to the learning opportunities provided. Alison intuitively understood that the same principle should guide her own decision making in thinking about how she would lead the school. Her decisions and actions should lead staff to feel positive, energized and in control of their own learning. The principle expressed her belief in leadership through listening, dialogue and working together, not top-down authority or external dictat.

In the classroom, the principle of *trust* implies that young people want to learn and will take up the teacher's invitations to engage with enthusiasm and commitment if they find activities relevant, purposeful and meaningful to them, and if the classroom conditions are supportive of their learning. If children refuse the invitation or appear to be inhibited in their learning, this basic position of trust means that teachers automatically re-evaluate their choices and practices in order to try to understand what might be hindering the children's engagement. Applying this principle to the leadership task, Alison trusted that staff did not need to be told what to do. She trusted that, if a sufficiently supportive environment could be created within the whole-school community, then, as active thinkers and learners in their own right, staff would take positive steps to develop their practice, without her pre-determining what these steps would be. While she felt it was important for everyone to have a sense of 'where we were heading as a school', in terms of a broad vision, the actual practices would be developed by the teachers themselves, in partnership with Alison, the children and the whole-school community.

Thirdly, the principle of *everybody* asserts, in the classroom, teachers' fundamental responsibility and commitment to acting in the interests of everybody, rather than in the interests of particular individuals, or groups of learners. The principle also recognizes that learning has a collective as well as an individual dimension. Teachers work to build a learning community, encouraging children to support and help one another: everybody must be valued, accepted, respected, everybody must feel that they belong, everybody must be recognized as having a unique contribution to make, everybody can learn with and from everybody else. In her leadership of the school, Alison's aspiration was to create a whole-school community where all adult members would also experience a strong sense of belonging: a community where teaching colleagues would be informed and excited by educational theory and would see themselves as lifelong learners.

Alison brought these insights, convictions and principles with her to Wroxham, to the task of leading the school. They embodied both the kind of school she hoped to create and the style of leadership she believed was needed in order to create it. Her approach was based on the hypothesis that staff learning would be the key to transforming children's learning capacities, and that similar conditions would be necessary for both. However, this being her first headship, she had yet to discover how these ideas and principles would translate into the practice of leadership in the complex hustle and bustle of everyday life in school.

Creating Learning without Limits: new research questions

We set out to study developments taking place in the school, guided by Alison's vision, as the school community lived and worked together over a period of two years. Specifically, we wanted to find out what strategies and practices were found to be effective in building this alternative approach to whole-school development. How did Alison go about creating a developmental and sustainable approach to building the learning capacity of teachers and children? How did she communicate her purposes and approach to the school community? How did members of staff take on board and work with the key ideas and principles of *Learning without Limits*? How did their classroom practices evolve? How did Alison manage the apparent tension between maintaining her own not-for-sale principles and offering staff the freedom to do their own thinking and develop their own practice as they thought best? What problems and challenges did staff encounter? How did they all, including Alison, mediate and fulfil statutory requirements? How did Alison sustain courage and belief in her approach, while swimming against the tide of national policy? What did the community learn – and what could we learn from them – about how to create learning without limits?

How the research was carried out

Details of our research approach can be found in Appendix B. Briefly, data collection took place over two and a half years, and was divided into three phases. In the first phase we explored in a relatively open-ended way what was happening in the school and what different members of the school community thought about these developments. We talked with teachers, observed lessons, recorded people's thinking about new practices and collected documentary information. The headteacher kept a reflective journal of events that she saw as significant, and also discussed her actions, strategies and developments in interview with a member of the university-based research team.

In the second phase, teachers were invited to carry out their own individual enquiries, focused on specific developments in their practice. We hoped that these individual enquiries would enable us to probe in more depth teachers' thinking, and the reasons underlying their decision-making. We encouraged teachers to follow up on current pressing questions arising from their everyday practice, rather than devising special projects which they would not ordinarily plan. We observed lessons and talked with the teachers afterwards about their purposes, the thinking that guided their actions, their evaluation of how well their purposes were being achieved and what they felt they were learning. We also talked with children to hear their perspectives on what was happening in the classroom, and with the parents of these children to find out what they thought of the changes taking place. Alison continued keeping her reflective journal and discussing issues arising in interviews.

Our intention was to work alongside the headteacher and staff group as they developed their approach together. We wanted to document for them the development of their thinking and practice as it occurred in the ordinary and everyday events in their school lives. We were very careful not to introduce ideas, opinions, or understandings of our own, or to offer advice or guidance: we wanted to elicit and probe the thinking of the staff. Our role was to offer a framework for reflection in interviews, methodological support to help them to design their individual teacher enquiries, and assistance in collecting data for these enquiries. All interview transcripts and observation field notes were shared with individual members of staff. In the third phase we formally analysed all the data, shared our preliminary analyses of each teacher's story, and also shared our draft writing and interpretations with them.

The Wroxham team during the research period

Table 1.1 outlines the Wroxham staff participating in case studies, and the year groups they were working with during the period of the research. The teachers' names are their real names and are used throughout the rest of the book. The children's names are pseudonyms.

Table 1.1 Wroxham staff participating in case studies

Year group	Age of children	Class teacher
Year 1	5–6 years	Cheryl
Year 2	6–7 years	Sophie
Year 3	7–8 years	Darrelle
Year 4	8–9 years	Martyn
Year 5	9–10 years	Jo
Year 6	10–11 years	Simon (deputy head)
Headteacher		Alison

Note: Teaching staff are referred to by their real names, but all the children have been given pseudonyms.

The unfolding story

In the next chapter, we draw on Alison's recollections and previous publications to explore how she approached the task of leadership when she first arrived at the school. Subsequent chapters take up our research story from that point. In Chapter 3 we explore the developments in thinking and practice of individual members of the teaching team during the research period and the common elements of practice that they felt were significant. In Chapter 4 we consider the focus of the teaching team on work to foster particular kinds of relationships with children that were fundamental to their work in school. In Chapter 5 we look in detail at the nature of the leadership task and the range of strategies employed in nurturing and sustaining the developments that were taking place. In Chapter 6 we review what we have learned from the Wroxham community about creating learning without limits. We contrast the distinctive approach to school improvement at Wroxham with the approach sponsored by the standards agenda, explore the relevance of our research for others and consider what lies ahead.

By the time the research began, Alison had already been at Wroxham for two years. In order to understand developments that took place over the next two years, we need to be aware of the foundations upon which those subsequent developments were built. We therefore turn first to the early period of Alison's headship at Wroxham and look at some of the developments in practice at that time. We consider if and how the principles outlined in this chapter were reflected in Alison's early actions and initiatives and how she began to communicate her vision to staff.

2 Laying foundations

Early days at Wroxham

In this chapter we explore what went on, in the early period of Alison's headship, that helped to lay the foundations for an alternative approach to school improvement, one inspired by commitment to creating better ways for everybody to live, work and learn together in an environment free from determinist beliefs about ability. In Chapter 1, we identified the *Learning without Limits* purposes and principles that Alison brought with her to Wroxham and that informed both her vision of what the school might become and her leadership. These principles provided Alison with ideas about the kind of leadership practices that might be appropriate but, as we acknowledged, she had no ready-made blueprint for how to enable a school to develop in the direction of her vision. She began her headship determined to resist the approach to school improvement, set by the standards agenda, to which schools have been subject over the last twenty years. In a paper published some years later, she expressed her conviction that school and teacher development needed to be managed in an empowering way:

> For too long external threat has been the central method of trying to improve school performance. This did not work for our school when it was failing. What our children and teachers needed was to be trusted again and to find their voice so that together learning could become exciting, challenging and joyous.
>
> (Peacock 2006: 258)

Alison was determined, right from the start, to work collaboratively, to encourage people by every means possible to be full and active participants in the reconstruction of a flourishing learning community. Within such a community, Alison believed, the learning of the staff group could become a significant means of enhancing children's learning. While it took courage to pursue her alternative path, Alison was aware that she would be given support from the local authority, from the governing body and from within the senior leadership team, so she would not be alone in facing the challenges ahead. Even before the headship interview, she had contacted the Head of the School Advisory and Inspection team to request assurance that, should she be successful in her application, the local authority would support her approach to school improvement. Then, in the first few weeks of her headship, a new Chair of Governors was elected, a business woman and parent governor, who had been a member of the appointing committee. The enthusiastic, skilled support of this person at this critical time for Alison's leadership was an important positive factor. A second crucial appointment followed: a new deputy headteacher, Simon Putman, was appointed in February 2003 and took up his post after Easter. When Simon first visited the school, Alison recalled their discussions as 'a meeting of minds'. Simon had previously worked in a London borough as a special needs coordinator; he firmly believed in the importance of raising children's self-esteem and in continually 'keeping the door open' for all children, including those seen as challenging. His enthusiasm and energy significantly supported the existing leadership team.

In this chapter we focus on some key strategies and initiatives that the staff group developed together as they began to build a new future for the school, and try retrospectively to understand how the foundations for creating learning without limits were embodied in these strategies. Initially, approaches and practices were developed intuitively in response to the immediacy of particular situations and challenges. As Alison acknowledged in an account of this early period, it was often only in retrospect that she could reflect on and notice the principles at work in her spontaneous decision making:

> The business of school leadership is so demanding and all consuming that it is a rare luxury to reflect on the process. Indeed, in those first years of headship there was precious little time to sit back and think about why actions were taken. Whilst in the process of rapid change, decisions were taken from the heart with little or no conscious regard of the deep rooted values and influences that impacted upon the process. It is only now with the help of a second research project [*Creating Learning without Limits*] that the process of leadership for change is becoming clearer.
>
> (Peacock 2006: 253)

Yet, with hindsight, it is clear that key messages were being communicated to staff and pupils from her very first day as headteacher. For her first whole-school assembly she sat on a stool with a brightly patterned cloth bag on her shoulder, and read to the children from a book called *The Huge Bag of Worries*; she told them that she herself had lots of worries as their new headteacher, and explained that the bag contained cards with a variety of messages, including: 'I am worried I will get lost in my new school', 'I am worried that there will be times when I won't know what to do', 'I am worried people will not come and talk to me'. One by one children offered to come up and take a card out of her bag and read it aloud. The children responded to each card by offering Alison advice until her bag of worries was empty and she was able to jump up and say how much better she felt. This small but significant first step is an example of how Alison signalled to both children and adults that she did not have a blueprint for change, that she valued everybody's ideas, and that there was a great deal to be gained from everybody in the school community, including the children, working in partnership.

Circle group meetings

The same message was given formal, institutional expression in a significant whole-school initiative that was established under the leadership of Simon, the new deputy head. The idea of introducing weekly, mixed-age circle group meetings emerged from a staff discussion about how to make more real and meaningful the invitation to everyone to give voice to their ideas, to participate in and contribute to decisions that would affect their lives in school. Unlike an elected (and thereby selective) school council, circle group meetings included *everybody*, all the adults (teachers, teaching assistants, governors, volunteers) and all the children in the school. In this way, the meetings aimed to reduce hierarchies (between adults with different roles, between adults and children, and between children) by stressing everybody's right to be heard and the value of everybody's contribution. The children were welcomed as equal partners in the Wroxham community; as such they needed to know what was happening in school just as much as the adults. Including children from every year group in each circle group was intended to help increase empathy and understanding between children of different ages, and to show that even the youngest children could be trusted to have something worthwhile to contribute.

The meetings took place every Tuesday morning for fifteen minutes just before playtime. Class lists were used to assign children to a group; on average 26 children aged between 5 and 11 attended each group meeting. Adults and children participated on an equal footing: the meeting began with everyone sitting on the floor together, in a circle. Initially Alison supported the process by providing a weekly agenda which was shared across the school and included suggestions for a warm-up game, news, points for discussion and a closing game. At first, meetings were led by staff and discussions focused on a range of practical issues that arose, week by week, with the priority being to build a shared understanding of issues from the different perspectives of younger and older children. Decisions were taken, for example, on premises development, and new playground equipment, sometimes following a ballot and sometimes after several weeks of discussion and reflection. Topics for circle group meetings soon moved beyond management issues and it became commonplace for discussions about teaching and learning to appear on the agenda. For instance, plans for a maths evening, when families would come into school to be taught by the children, were developed in circle group meetings. Similarly, discussions were held about new initiatives such as the introduction of a school radio station and café and ideas for new games to play on the playground.

Year 6 children were given the responsibility for making notes of the discussions and decisions during the meetings. They used these notes to feed back to the other circle group leaders so that everybody knew what was happening in the other groups. This provided a chance for all the adults involved to notice how ably the children responded to the trust invested in them. By mid-2005, when the research period began, the circle group meetings were being led entirely by Year 6 children. Every child in this year group took part, working in teams of four, who divided the tasks of leading the circle groups between them. Taking on these considerable responsibilities gave every Year 6 child the opportunity to develop skills of leadership and empathy. They were trusted to plan and structure meetings appropriately and to manage behaviour in the group. Observations by members of the research team showed that they were well able to carry out this leadership role: treating others respectfully, giving younger children time to articulate their ideas, supporting less confident children by encouraging them, offering to return to them later for suggestions they wished to make, and suggesting adjustments to seating in the circle in order to give an individual more space.

The circle group strategy offered the teaching team an authentic context in which to experience and appreciate the importance of listening to children, to build respect for and trust in their responses, and to be surprised by the quality of children's thinking. During the research period, Simon identified as hugely important the development of a whole-school community through circle group meetings: 'I believe in circle time more than anything else really, to get to know the children and what they want.' Circle group meetings laid the basis for a culture of democracy, helping to reduce hierarchies and build partnerships as the children and adults shared discussions and reached decisions. They encouraged everybody to think for themselves, to take initiatives rather than simply to implement something that had been imposed on them. By enabling everybody to contribute, the Wroxham team was building a sense of belonging to an increasingly thriving community.

Learning review meetings

Another significant initiative at this time was a reorganization of the ways in which the teachers of Years 5 and 6 monitored children's progress in learning.

'Learning review meetings' were established, at which individual children, their parents, the class teacher and headteacher met together for a collaborative, formative discussion, focusing on each child's progress and achievements, and on how she or he could best be supported in the future. The purpose of these meetings was to build a shared understanding of each child's progress and aspirations for the future, from the child's perspective. The emphasis on listening and responding to the child's point of view meant that the adults present, both teachers and parents, could look at learning in the round, as a personal, living experience; they heard an account of the human, emotional dimension of learning, rather than the targets the child had achieved or the levels reached.

The learning review meetings were held twice a year, in the autumn and spring terms, and lasted for about twenty minutes. They were held in the headteacher's room, during or after the school day; Alison attended all the meetings, thus learning more about each child's experience and progress. In preparation for the meetings, the teachers devised an open-ended questionnaire covering all aspects of the children's learning and well-being, in order to elicit their personal views of their successes, their worries, the things they found challenging, their need for support, or changes in their support, their hopes for the future. Each child discussed the completed questionnaire, in confidence, with the class teacher, and selected the issues and areas to be discussed at the learning review meeting. Alison recalled that the children responded to this new procedure with enthusiasm; they took full advantage of the opportunity to do a thorough, serious, honest review of their learning.

In the learning review meetings children were able to participate not as passive subjects, whose learning was to be measured and judged by others, but as responsible, active learners, with a positive part to play in creating their own futures. The format of the meetings encouraged everybody to join a conversation about learning, speaking as equal partners, sharing their own knowledge and understanding, and contributing ideas about future progress and how best to support it. The meetings were not used to set targets, nor were levels of attainment or tracking data used to assess improvement. The meetings were used to agree on ways forward and actions for the future, which were recorded in notes of the meeting; each subsequent meeting was a continuation of what became an ongoing dialogue between the participants, based on an open culture of sharing, guided by the principles of reciprocity and respect.

These learning review meetings laid the foundations for a different approach to monitoring and accountability: a team approach based on the need to understand and appreciate individual learners. The meetings enabled the headteacher to keep a close and watchful eye on every child's learning, giving her deeper insights than could be gained through hours of classroom observation, or tracking performance data through levels; she was able to monitor the degree of consistency and coherence as the children moved from class to class. Learning review meetings also generated the opportunity for the teaching staff to see the value of working in partnership with parents, to realize how thoughtfully children could discuss their personal experiences of learning, and to recognize the importance of children's active participation in the process of learning review.

Faculty teams

In many primary schools, individual teachers take on leadership responsibility for a single subject area of the curriculum, such as literacy, science or music. At Wroxham, this way of working was set aside; in its place, faculty teams were created with the explicit purpose of building a partnership approach to curriculum development. The faculty teams included both more and less experienced teachers and teaching assistants, joined by governors, who brought their out-of-school experience to the teams. In this way, the faculty teams provided a structure within which every member of staff could participate in and contribute to curriculum planning, and, in the process, develop their own expertise in a cluster of related aspects of primary education.

The faculty teams took responsibility for three major areas of the curriculum; the staff chose which team to join from a Humanities Faculty, a Creative Faculty and a Citizenship Faculty (see Table 2.1). Their meetings were held three times a term, for two hours after school, with refreshments provided, each team working from the whole-school development plan. Their work included collecting relevant examples of children's work, identifying practices that might stimulate debate and discussion, both from within and beyond the school, planning a diary of opportunities and worthwhile experiences for both children and staff, advising on courses people might want to attend, and identifying visitors who might be invited to work with the children. Staff prepared lessons that other faculty members were invited to attend, creating opportunities for cross-faculty discussion after the lesson. The teams planned how to

Table 2.1 Faculty teams: a team approach to subject leadership

Humanities Faculty	Creative Faculty	Citizenship Faculty
History	Play	Forest school
Geography	Music	Extended school
Languages	Dance	Lunch-time play
Design and Technology	Drama	Religious education
Mathematics	English	Personal, Social and Health Education
	ICT	Science
	Art	Physical Education and Games
		Global Education

share their developing ideas with others in the school community; they made use of faculty team notice boards in the staffroom to ask for help (such as contributions to a display), to issue invitations, and to publicize special events.

This team approach to curriculum leadership replaced the more usual practice of individual subject leaders observing, monitoring and evaluating the teaching of their colleagues. The premise for this change was that a top-down approach to teacher development, where more expert and experienced teachers judge the performance of colleagues and identify areas for improvement, limits everybody's learning. Professional learning should not be concerned with identifying and remedying deficits in performance, but with deepening understanding of children's learning and developing practices informed by these new understandings. To be continually learning is everybody's responsibility; all members of staff should have opportunities to learn, to develop new practices, and to share their growing expertise. The faculty teams provided rich opportunities for such learning and sharing: within the teams, members could learn from one another, challenge each other, identify questions to investigate, share their discoveries and put their understanding to good use.

The supportive, empowering structure of the faculty teams set out to harness the energy and resources of the whole staff team, fostering creativity and openness. More confident or experienced members of staff supported less experienced members, and valued what they were doing. The structure encouraged everybody to reconsider what kinds of learning experiences are most worthwhile; faculty team members inspired and supported one another in planning opportunities for children that would be meaningful and motivating.

In parallel with learning review meetings, the establishment of faculty teams embodied a shift in the school-wide management of accountability. In place of teacher performance across the curriculum being monitored and evaluated individually, faculty teams took on shared responsibility for three distinct but interrelated aspects of teaching and learning. First, they assumed responsibility for the quality of experiences and opportunities offered to children in their particular curriculum areas; secondly, they took on the task of monitoring the quality of children's learning in each of these areas. Thirdly, their collaborative approach was a way of nourishing and sustaining their own learning as they shared the outcomes of their small-scale initiatives. The foundations were being laid for the whole teaching team to work together in the interests of the learning of everybody – both teachers and children.

Continuing professional development across the school

The commitment of the leadership team to building a new culture of learning for adults as well as for children was reflected in sustained support for continuing professional development for all members of the teaching team. This support across the school was based on trust, on the belief that people could be empowered to think for themselves, to find their own way. The staff group were trusted to take up the opportunities they were offered to engage in worthwhile, purposeful learning.

A striking example of this commitment was the substantial support given to four teaching assistants, who embarked on foundation degrees in education at the University of Hertfordshire. The teaching assistants were released from the school for one day a week, on full pay, to attend their courses; when they were under pressure to complete assignments, they were given study leave, again on full pay. This generous provision was fully supported by the governing body, who were convinced that this kind of sustained further study would benefit the whole school community. Members of staff were encouraged to learn from each other; each teaching assistant was assigned a mentor from the teaching staff, and their work together became a channel for the dissemination of the insights they were gaining through their small-scale classroom-based enquiries. All four teaching assistants were awarded an honours degree; three went on to complete a Graduate Teacher programme, based at Wroxham, and are now teaching in Hertfordshire schools.

Additional support was given by the headteacher, who took a personal interest in each student's studies; this was a source of useful feedback on the emerging culture of learning, and on areas ripe for future development. This consistent approach to school-wide continuing professional development, supplemented by the work of the faculty teams, created conditions in which the whole staff group could be enriched by the thinking and developing prac- tices of their colleagues; their support for children's learning was energized and enhanced by their own learning.

Enlivening learning

While these various initiatives were gradually becoming embedded in the day- by-day practice of the school, there were other changes in curriculum provi- sion and planning. Staff were encouraged to prioritize opportunities for learning that children would find purposeful, meaningful and rewarding. Inviting displays and role play areas were set up; collections of interesting objects were offered as starting points for exploration and enquiry. Visiting sculptors, writers, dancers and musicians were invited to work with children and staff to enliven learning.

Creativity was encouraged in responding to external initiatives. One such initiative (DfES 2003a), aimed at fostering 'Speaking and Listening', unexpect- edly stimulated the invention and installation of Wroxham Radio station. Along with the strategy documents, the school was sent a box of resources, to support a series of activities for staff. Without feeling constrained to work through every activity in the box, the staff group came together to examine the resources. Alison recalled that an animated discussion ensued about what was already happening in school in these curriculum areas, which kindled creative thinking about what more could be done. As people debated how to increase opportunities for sustained, purposeful speaking and listening, Simon suggested an in-house radio station. Staff and children took up the idea and discussed possibilities in their circle group meetings, where many ambitious suggestions were made. Key Stage 2 children, 7- to 11-year-olds, took part in workshop training led by an ex-BBC radio journalist, during which they explored how radio programmes are structured, and how to combine music and speech. They thought about the impact of radio on the audience and learned how presenters use language to catch the audience's attention. The radio station, a purpose-built bench with a mixer-board, microphones and computer, was housed in the school library, next to the dining area, recently transformed into the Wroxham café. The whole school assembled to witness the launch of Wroxham radio; subsequently the 10- and 11-year-old children organized and controlled the broadcasting programme of lively music, brief commentaries, and announcements of activities happening around school, to entertain and inform each other at lunchtime. This initiative encouraged people to see the possibility of purposeful and rewarding activity, managed by the children, outside the classroom, with minimal adult direction.

Sometimes teaching staff were offered interesting resources as a provocation for inspiring children's learning. One weekend, for example, several weeks into her headship, Alison came across a cardboard box full of Victorian glass bottles encrusted with mud at a car boot sale. The vendor explained that he was a builder and had dug the bottles up when working on a roundabout in East London. Knowing that the Year 2 children were studying Victorian history, Alison bought the bottles, seeing an opportunity for enlivening learning. At that time Jo, who we will meet during the research period as a Year 5 teacher, was teaching Year 2. When she arrived in school that Monday morning, she found the box of muddy bottles in her room. Alison suggested that a really interesting historical enquiry could take place if the class were to investigate the bottles. Jo, then in her second year of teaching, found the prospect both exciting and challenging. Several days later she presented Alison with a plan for a variety of activities that would involve the children working in groups to clean the bottles and generate questions about them. Alison recalls how, when she visited the classroom, the whole class was busily engaged with bowls of soapy water and old toothbrushes examining genuine Victorian artefacts. The atmosphere in the room was electric: the children were bursting with excitement and news about what they were discovering. This activity inspired several weeks of lessons, and the children's work on the enquiry – photographs, charts, measurements, calculations, writing – was commended by HMI during that term's inspection visit. Teachers from across the school were urged to go and see what was taking place, to see for themselves how the provision of an open-ended experience enabled all the children to participate with high levels of motivation, to see powerful learners at work, and to celebrate the way in which this teacher had created the conditions for worthwhile learning.

Informal one-to-one conversations also often had worthwhile outcomes. For instance, having discovered an old apple tree, loaded with fruit, in a remote corner of the grounds, Alison said to Sarah, who worked with the 4- and 5-year-olds, 'Wouldn't it be lovely if the children could go out and investigate all the different trees and then just happen to come across a tree laden with apples? Wouldn't it be fantastic for them to pick the apples?' The suggestion was not made didactically or with the expectation that it must be taken up, nor were specific learning outcomes identified. The invitation was offered and then left hanging. A couple of days later, a 5-year-old child came to Alison's office to offer her some freshly cooked apple crumble. The children had explored the grounds and had collected bags full of apples, which were duly washed, peeled, chopped and cooked. 'It was so exciting,' Alison recalled, 'because they'd found this treasure. They'd been looking at all these different trees . . . and then suddenly there were all these apples!' Similarly, convinced that the richer the experience, the richer the learning that was likely to result, the staff sought out unusual resources to stimulate children's play.

Bringing the curriculum to life in these ways laid foundations for a rich, open, multifaceted view of learning, where outcomes could not be pre-specified. They helped staff to appreciate more fully how the quality of their provision affected the children's capacity to learn, sometimes in new or unexpected contexts. Small steps such as these were significant in that they enabled the staff team to move beyond an overriding concern with attainment targets, learning objectives and levels. By their responses the children demonstrated the different kinds of unexpected learning that can take place when children take more control: the children started to surprise their teachers with their enthusiasm, competence, energy and expertise. In Chapter 3 we describe how the staff team's work developed over time, and how their expectations of children continued to rise.

Conclusion

These early structures and initiatives were not just worthwhile developments in their own right. In retrospect, we can recognize how together they were laying foundations for the development of a flourishing school community free from determinist beliefs about ability. The circle group meetings, learning review meetings and initiatives to enliven the curriculum were helping to create conditions in which children's thirst for and active involvement in their own learning could be restored, nurtured and strengthened. They were also creating conditions in which children could surprise their teachers and themselves, inviting the development of richer and more complex ways of thinking and talking about learning than the reductive language and concepts of ability and levels. These initiatives, along with the faculty teams and support for continuing professional development, were also laying foundations for the development of a strong, cohesive teaching team with a collective commitment to ongoing professional learning across the teaching staff as a whole.

The structures and activities, in themselves, were not as important as what they set in motion: the emergence of a new way of working together, a new way of thinking about learners and a new approach to learning and teaching. Other structures and activities could have been used to further the same ends. Increased opportunities for thinking for oneself, for thinking with colleagues, for taking time for reflection and discussion, as provided by these structures and strategies, enabled the staff group to explore new territory together; they encouraged a willingness to tussle with complexity, to keep learning. They helped people to see new possibilities rather than familiar certainties, to develop a sense that anything could happen, that the future is built from what happens in the present. They encouraged a shift towards a more open view of learning, to see that worthwhile learning is often unpredictable. Team discussions provided a forum for dialogue, where staff began to talk together about children's powers as learners, and the depth of their engagement in learning that is relevant and meaningful to them.

With the benefit of hindsight, we can appreciate how the deeply rooted principles that Alison brought with her to Wroxham, as outlined in Chapter 1, have been embodied in these structures and initiatives, not just to support the learning of children but that of adults too. The principle of co-agency – working in partnership, encouraging people to think for themselves, to take initiatives, to do their own learning and to play a full and active part in the development of the learning community – is a common theme throughout the various initiatives described. The principle of everybody can be clearly seen at work in the circle group meetings, where everyone takes part on an equal footing and everyone is given a voice; in the faculty teams, which include all members of the teaching staff plus governors; and in the approach to supporting continuing professional development, which recognizes the need to support the learning of all members of the teaching team, not just those with qualified teacher status. Most importantly, perhaps, trust in people's capacity to grow and learn, given supportive conditions, clearly lay at the heart of the approach to leadership from the very first days. Rather than imposing her ideas or specifying the practices that would reflect them, Alison trusted that structures and strategies progressively put in place by the staff team would provide the experiences and stimulate the insights that would guide people in directions implied by the principles without precisely defining how her colleagues should enact them, or what the outcomes should be. The staff group were given the freedom to think for themselves, to find their own ways of working within the new structures and their own solutions to the challenges they met. The new strategies and initiatives worked together to create a sense of shared endeavour, and a collaborative environment that supported the learning of everybody; all this, Alison reasoned, would generate a new energy – the energy of hope.

Our first preliminary answer, then, to the question of how Alison communicated her vision to staff was that she did so by ensuring that new structures and initiatives put in place by the whole staff team embodied particular kinds of rich learning opportunities, for staff and children. She then trusted them to construct their own meanings and be inspired to do their own learning through participation in those experiences. In the next chapter, we explore developments in the thinking and practices of teachers who agreed to take part in the research, which began two years into Alison's headship, as they continued building their own ways of working with children within this environment. We consider if and how these developments grew from the foundations described in this chapter and how they contributed to creating learning without limits.

It is important to emphasize that in using the word 'creating' we are not using a biblical metaphor, drawn from the Book of Genesis. Clearly the endeavour of creating a humane and equitable school cannot be completed in seven days, or even seven years. We use the term 'creating' to suggest a process of continuous development and continuous renewal, a process in which the moment when there is no more work to be done will simply never arrive. Creating learning without limits is a project with no discernible end-point. But the absence of a fixed end does not condemn those committed to this shared project to an infinite future of unfulfilment. As we shall see, in the Wroxham story so far, there have been, inevitably, struggles and difficulties, but also joy and exhilaration arising from a new shared sense of purpose coupled with many significant achievements. It is to these achievements that we now turn.

3   Extending freedom to learn

In this chapter, we fast forward to the research period to see what developments were taking place in the thinking and practices of members of the teaching staff. We focus in particular on our finding that, while each teacher's approach was distinctively individual, there was nevertheless a strong measure of agreement, among the teachers whose work we documented in detail, about what was important pedagogically and where they needed to direct their efforts in the development of their practice. There was agreement, for example, about the importance of listening to children, extending opportunities for choice, learning collaboratively, enlivening learning through authentic, relevant experiences, and involving children in assessing their own learning. As we shall see, because of this broad agreement, teachers were also able to join forces and create innovative projects that transcended the boundaries of individual classrooms and year groups. In this chapter we examine these common elements and explore their significance for the Wroxham teachers. Why did the teachers give such priority to these elements and make them a focus for their development work? How did this apparent consensus emerge, when everyone acknowledged that it was in no sense imposed? How did thinking and practice interact, for individual teachers, as they developed their own approaches? What part did the staff group *collectively* play in influencing developments? And how was the emerging consensus linked to the foundations described in Chapter 2 and to the general principles that underpinned Alison's leadership of the school and her vision for the development of practice?

Offering choices

One common element in the work of all the teachers was a commitment to offering children more choices in their learning. While most primary classrooms do offer children opportunities to choose – for example when they have completed set tasks, or in a particular period of time set aside each week – it is less usual to find choice playing an integral and increasing role in the way the classroom operates generally. At Wroxham, when teachers provided differentiated tasks (that is, tasks with different levels of challenge relating to the same topic, rather than tasks reflecting National Curriculum levels) children chose their own levels of work. They chose their own learning partners or groups, where to sit and whom to sit with. They chose when they were ready to move on to a new activity or felt confident enough to commence work independently, without an adult's support. They made their own choices of activities to pursue from a carousel of possibilities and, in some classes, they even chose whether or not to take up opportunities for additional individual support. Extending opportunities for choice went hand in hand with listening to children, inviting and enabling them to offer their ideas and shape their own experiences both in and out of the classroom. Even very young children were given considerable responsibility for decisions relating to their own learning and experiences in school. How might we understand the significance given to 'choice' by these teachers as an essential feature of classroom practice? How did it work as a strategy and how did the teachers build children's capacity to make wise and productive choices?

The strategy of offering children a choice of levels of work was being developed specifically as one important way of overcoming the problems that the teachers now associated with ability-based grouping and the allocation of differentiated tasks to identified groups and individuals by the teacher. Cheryl, for instance, who had moved away from grouping by ability relatively recently, recalled that the children in the lower-attaining group tended to lose faith in their abilities, developing a mindset of defeatism where they felt helpless ('I can't do it') unless an adult was there to help them. Ability grouping also affected the attitudes to learning of children in higher attaining groups, who tended to become competitive, and were reluctant to ask for help if they didn't understand. Cheryl explained: 'Even in the higher group, you can still have a little hierarchy of who's the cleverest in that group, and who's the slowest and who maybe shouldn't even be in this group.'

By offering a choice of work at different levels, it became possible to challenge and extend the learning of all children, without predetermining what any individual in the class might be capable of achieving and without communicating messages of differential worth or undermining children's belief in their own capabilities. So Jo, for example, an Advanced Skills Teacher who was working with 9- and 10-year-olds, routinely offered a range of tasks, in mathematics, at different levels of demand (at first she called these levels 'Back to Basics 1', 'Back to Basics 2', 'Consolidation' 'Challenge 1' and 'Challenge 2'). She trusted the children to choose their own level of work, and to change their minds if they discovered that their original choice was either too easy or too difficult. No one was limited to work at any particular level, and children frequently undertook tasks at more than one level during any given lesson. Children were also trusted to choose whom to sit with, and children freely chose partners and groups who were not doing work at the same level of challenge. Talk and collaboration were encouraged among partners seated together, whatever activities they were engaged in.

Simon's approach was somewhat different. Following a discussion with his Year 6 class, and just for mathematics, he had moved to a system of zones in the classroom, each offering a differentiated task, for example in relation to fractions. The children chose which zone to work in based on their sense of what level of challenge they wanted to give themselves in relation to a particular topic. This meant that children who were working on similar tasks were gathered in the same area, and so made it easier for Simon to target particular groups or individuals when help was needed with understanding particular concepts. It also allowed grouping patterns to be responsive to variations in individuals' confidence and skill in relation to different mathematical topics. However, there was less likelihood of creating the hierarchies associated with ability grouping, because the children made the choice of zone for themselves. It was they who decided the degree of challenge they felt ready to undertake in relation to a particular topic; they could choose to be in a different zone on different days, or move between zones in the same session, depending on how confident they felt tackling particular topics and tasks. There was no shame involved in moving to an easier zone, because children could also make the choice to move on to more challenging work when they felt ready.

These are sophisticated judgements, of course, requiring mature attitudes, self-appraisal and serious investment in learning, but the young people in these classes showed themselves to be well worthy of their teachers' trust that they would be able to achieve these states of mind with the right encouragement and support. Tom, for instance, in Simon's class, commented that sometimes a child can be a better judge of the level of work required than the teacher. 'Like you know what you can do and sometimes a teacher doesn't. So if a teacher thinks you're finding it hard and maybe you're not, you can do what you want and take control of your own learning.' Tina, a fellow classmate, insisted that her teacher's trust was well-placed: 'The teachers can trust us to choose the right work, because there's not much point just choosing work that is easy for you when you can do the harder work.' Simon recalled a student teacher who was observing his class for a week: 'He stayed in the room for a while and he couldn't believe that they could choose their work and different ways of doing things. And he said, "Why don't the lazy ones just do nothing?" And I said, "Well try and find me one. Try and find me a lazy kid . . . that doesn't want to learn."'

Simon stressed that, while he kept 'a watchful eye' on where children were going, it was very different from labelling children or groups. 'I haven't got groups. It's more like I know roughly who will choose that level of work and who wouldn't, and then again you can be surprised.' Both Simon and Jo saw it as a necessary and valuable learning process for young people gradually to build their confidence and ability to choose wisely through their teachers' interactions with them. Both talked with their classes about peer pressure and worked at helping them to develop the self-awareness needed not to be swayed by the choices of other children. They carefully observed how children were coping with the work they had chosen and talked to children individually about their decision making. The sophistication of their developing self-awareness in making choices of level of work is revealed in many other children's comments. For example, Petra said, 'It's up to you how you go. If you want to make it easier for yourself, then it's your learning that you're disrupting. If you want to challenge yourself, then it's you you're doing it for, it's not for anyone else. So it's up to you how you do it, but it's best to challenge yourself and do as best as you can in everything because you only get one shot.'

Martyn discovered that changing the way that the different levels were designated, in mathematics, helped to overcome some of the problems that children in his Year 4 class were experiencing in making wise choices. Initially he had named the three levels 'I need help,' 'Practice' and 'Challenge'. Finding that some of the children insisted on choosing 'Challenge' and then were discouraged when they found it too hard, he decided to rename the different levels 'Challenge 1/2/3'. The new names aptly embraced the principle that, whatever task was chosen, it should present a challenge to the learner. The children's reaction to this seemingly simple change was a revelation. No one minded selecting the first level of work when it was labelled Challenge 1. Success at Challenge 1 gave them the confidence to move on to Challenge 2. Again, young people in his class were able to articulate the benefits that they saw in having the opportunity to choose their own levels of work. John, for example, commented, 'You get to understand your learning better. I know which parts of work I can do and which parts I can't do, instead of just doing something because it has to be done.' Although Martyn had had doubts early on that children would be able to choose their own level of work, he was excited to see them becoming happier and more confident. Nevertheless, Martyn continued to question the efficacy of the strategy, and to compare the attainments of his current class with those in his previous school. He wanted to be sure that offering a choice of task was benefiting the children's learning as well as their sense of confidence and well-being. While many of the children were good at evaluating their level of work, there were still a few who struggled. He said, 'The whole idea of them choosing their level hopefully boosts their esteem and encourages them to work, but there are still those children who will basically copy and those who will rely on an adult to support them. So it's not perfect.'

Cheryl thought it was a very big step to hand over such a degree of control to Year 1 children. She worried at first that they would not make the choices that she felt they should, that some children would choose easy options and would not be sufficiently pushed. She experimented initially with offering children a choice of different ways of expressing and representing their learning, from a carousel of possibilities. For example, when they were retelling the story of The Gingerbread Man, she gave them the choice of doing this through modelling with clay, through art or music, through rereading and re-enacting the story, or by writing on the computer. She came to see that 'choice' was not a strategy that she could simply add on to her existing approach but actually implied a fundamental reappraisal of how she was operating as a teacher. Over a period of a year, she observed and monitored how her children took up various opportunities to choose. In her own words, she 'took a step back, and let them have a bit more freedom', noticing that the less she directed proceedings herself, the more the children seemed to be able to do for themselves. She observed that what they learned seemed to mean more to them and they remembered it better when they had chosen and directed the activities, than when activities had been more tightly directed by her. She began to see that there was much to be gained from allowing space for the unanticipated and unexpected to happen. Her worries about children not being sufficiently pushed were gradually allayed as she saw how the children pushed themselves, when they had more freedom to pursue their own choices. 'Where we haven't pushed them and pushed them,' she commented, 'they do it naturally.'

Offering choices of levels of work was just one approach being explored by Wroxham teachers to cater for diversity within their classes. As we shall see when we look in more detail at their work to develop more authentic learning experiences, teachers were also working on extending opportunities for learning where outcomes were not tightly prespecified and children's learning was not articulated in terms of levels. However, their commitment to offering children a choice of levels of challenge, and to encouraging and enabling children to make choices in their learning more generally, reflected a growing, shared conviction that the opportunity to make choices was a necessary element of the conditions that nurture active, engaged, enthusiastic, intrinsically motivated learners. The teachers saw for themselves that when children were enabled to make choices this could and did lead to many subtle, positive changes: in their attitudes to learning, in their emotional and intellectual investment in classroom activities, in their positive sense of themselves as learners, their sense of heightened trust in their relationships with their teachers and other adults, and in their increased sense of importance, participation and belonging within the school community. These positive states of mind were so important, and the role of choice in them so potentially crucial that, despite some personal reservations, there was general agreement that this was a strategy worth working at. As Martyn explained, the staff group worked together, trying things out and reflecting on the outcomes: 'We have a really good staff who are open to new ideas and new ways of working, and if something doesn't work, we will just think about it, and think how we can change it, how we can work with that rather than just give up on it all together'.

Listening to children

The commitment to extending choice was also intimately bound up with another equally important focus of Wroxham teachers' practice and develop-ment work, namely listening to children and taking on board their ideas, thoughts and feelings – not just about their learning but all aspects of their life in school. Darrelle in particular encouraged sustained whole-class discussion and debate in her classroom. The time that she set aside for children to express their ideas, and respond to those of others, helped them to feel that their ideas were important, and were valued by their teacher. Sometimes they became so absorbed in their discussions that they did not notice that it was playtime.

Giving specific choices was one very practical way of encouraging children to express preferences and act on them. Increasingly, children were given opportunities not just to make their own selection from a range of activities offered by the teacher but also to contribute to the process of planning the tasks and activities to be undertaken by their class. Bath (2009), in a valuable study of how young children's participation in the early years can be enabled, notes the importance of distinguishing between the two kinds of involvement. She quotes Moss (2001: 17), who draws attention to the danger that 'listening to children can become a subtle but effective way to control them'. She argues that it is important that children's participation should not be limited simply to activities and structures that have already been decided upon, but should enable them actually to 'influence the overall organization set by the teacher' (2001: 33).

An example of participation of this second kind was provided by Sophie, who described how she involved her Year 2 class in planning experiences around the work of the author, Roald Dahl. The topic had grown from the children's enthusiasm while reading Roald Dahl's books, followed by a visit to the Roald Dahl museum, where they had spent time in a replica of his writing hut, created their own characters, dressed up in costumes and played out stories. The following day, Sophie and the children discussed what they would like to learn more about in relation to Roald Dahl and what kinds of activities they would like to do. The list of activities they came up with is shown in Table 3.1.

The list was left displayed in the classroom, so that the children could continue adding to it, while Sophie planned the unit of work to ensure that the children's suggestions would also satisfy National Curriculum requirements. Sophie noticed how excited and enthusiastic the children were when they were engaged in activities that they themselves had suggested. The sense of

Table 3.1 Joint planning by Year 2 children and their class teacher

Character day, where the children could dress up as a Roald Dahl character.

Use ICT to make their own Golden Tickets.

Role-play area: to become Roald Dahl's writing hut.

Use patterns and textures to make their own Roly Poly birds from the Twits.

Use part of the story from the Twits to make a papier mache Mrs Twit who was attached to the ceiling.

Create their own characters; plan and write a story using their characters.

Write a poem about their favourite Roald Dahl characters.

Draw their own illustrations for Roald Dahl books.

Write their own dream bottles for the Big Friendly Giant.

Write a character description using a missing or wanted poster of a Roald Dahl character.

Use the internet to research Roald Dahl and quiz to find out what they had learned.

Create their own Roald Dahl passports, including facts they had learned about him.

shared power created by involving them in planning in this way seemed to heighten their investment in their learning. Indeed, Sophie felt that the joint planning and work around this topic had been a turning point with the challenging class she had taken over in her second year of teaching. As we shall see in more detail in the next chapter, these children began the year with very negative feelings about how they sensed they were perceived as learners, which were expressed in their behaviour. Sophie thought that the activities around Roald Dahl had created a real sense of ownership, and had led to further suggestions, including the idea of creating a class book for Alison who had accompanied them to the museum. Everybody was able to contribute a piece of work to the class book, which, as we write, is still displayed in Alison's office.

By extending opportunities for children to make choices, for them to be listened to and have a say in what and how they learn, teachers were creating conditions in which children were increasingly able to *feel* and to *be* in control of their learning. Simon talked about the important part that he felt choice could play in helping to engage the few children – 'you're always going to get a handful' – who expressed reluctance to write. Offering choices was a way of 'keeping the doors open' and giving them as many opportunities to succeed as possible. If the class was working on writing plays, for instance, and they expressed resistance to that, might they prefer to do a story board? Or type it out? Or dictate their ideas? Would they like to write a play about a topic of their choice? Through offering choice, the teacher could retain control of the situation but also enable the child to exercise some control. 'Actually you're going together,' Simon commented, 'and it's true learning together' because, as he explained, the teacher learns more about the children's preferences; the children discover that they can genuinely have a say in their learning; and by making a choice among the options suggested, they end up engaging in worth-while writing tasks, along the lines of the teacher's original intentions, but negotiated between them.

Another area where, in some of the older classes, children were listened to and trusted to make their own choices was in relation to participation in additional support groups for literacy and numeracy. One DfES sponsored initiative, during the research period, involved setting up support groups, led by teaching assistants, to boost the achievement of children who were 'falling behind' (DfES 2003b). There were 'Wave 2' booster groups for children who were thought unlikely to reach national standards at the end of Year 6 (Level 4), and 'Wave 3' support for individuals designated as having special educational needs, who were considered to require ongoing one-to-one programmes with a view to accelerating their learning. In many schools, children were allocated to these groups on the basis of attainment, and participation was not usually optional. At Wroxham, in the Year 5 and Year 6 classes, by contrast, teaching assistants and class teachers talked with the children about what additional support groups were available and what they offered. The children then made their own choice to opt in or out. It was felt to be crucial to the success of their participation in the groups that they made this active commitment themselves.

Ironically, the decision to opt *out* provided for some children a significant stimulus to learning. A Year 5 child, for example, who was, by his own confession, 'struggling' with maths, opted not to avail himself of this support. Despite his class teacher's initial anxiety, his decision was respected, and his choice to stay in the classroom with his teacher was taken seriously, as an appropriate use of his responsibility for his own learning. Within a very short period (weeks rather than months) there appeared to be a change in his attitude to the subject, as his teacher observed his growing confidence. His progress as a learner of mathematics was dramatic.

Handing over more control to the children did not imply an abdication of responsibility on the part of the teachers. Rather it was a redirection of expertise and skill towards laying the foundations for this sense of control, in the belief that a greater sense of control would in turn lead to better learning. Year 5 teacher Jo, who was studying for a master's degree at the time, wrote in her thesis, 'Once you begin to trust the learners and regard them as the "experts" in their own learning, you begin to realize that you may have been limiting them by trying to control the work they engage in' (Smith 2007: 18). When children are in control, they are arguably better able to make use of their existing knowledge, skills and experiences to extend and develop their existing powers. They are better able to sustain concentration, to think and reason, to persist in the face of difficulties, to work at and find their own solutions to problems. Like Cheryl, whose changing practice we described earlier, other teachers' accounts of their own development during the period of the research often cited, as part of the process, the progressive loosening of the reins of teacher control, as they saw how enthusiastically children responded, and how the quality of their learning was enhanced when they were trusted to take more responsibility.

This was certainly Jo's experience when she decided to give her 9-year-olds a personal notebook that they could use at any time and for any purpose to support their learning. The idea evolved initially as a solution to a practical problem: how to keep a record, from one day to the next, of ideas, rough work and jottings that children were making on their white boards. Once the children took ownership of their notebooks, however, and began to trust that, as long as they were used to enhance their learning, they really were free to define their own purposes for them, the use of the notebooks took off in many unexpected ways. Jo was full of admiration and respect for the children's purposefulness and ingenuity. 'They use the notebooks *incredibly* well,' she said. The availability of a notebook for recording ideas, note taking and doodling provided freedom to learn in a way that was so simple yet vital. Indeed, Jo's animated defence of the value of doodling recalls an exhibition held at Kettle's Yard, Cambridge (2006), which amply demonstrated the power of thinking through drawing, including doodling, as an exploratory and explanatory tool used by scientists, historians, philosophers and surgeons, among others.

The notebooks in Jo's class not only became a real learning tool but, for some children, they became the repository for some of their most important and deeply felt learning, the place to pursue their personal interests and lines of enquiry. For example, Derek was captivated by language and used his notebook to keep a record of new sophisticated words he liked the sound of, with the dictionary definitions alongside. Words such as 'rhetorical' were written and overwritten decoratively several times, as if to embed the word in his mind. He created a long list of mathematical terms that he joyfully collected during maths lessons. He recorded an ever-increasing anthology of scientific facts and lists of information about how to construct different types of text such as narrative poetry and persuasive writing. Derek was deeply proud of his notebooks and the recognition that they afforded him within the class group. He would announce to visitors to the class that his notebooks were 'famous'. When books were completed, it was entirely the choice of the child whether to throw them away, having served their purpose, or keep them for future reference. Derek's sense of their significance was revealed when he decided to donate his completed books to the research team.

Learning together

A third common element was a commitment to developing the power of learning as a social activity. Children were not merely seated in pairs or groups but were actively encouraged to learn from and with one another. They were expected – and enabled – to listen to, value, use and build on the ideas of others in their own learning, to share their own ideas and to give help when asked. Even when engaged in an individual task, such as a piece of personal writing, children worked with a partner or in a group. They learned to use each other's resources to help generate ideas, build confidence, support each other's thinking, provide an audience, offer feedback on work in progress. Partnerships and groupings were not selected on the basis of judgements of supposed ability or attainment; indeed, this was another area where, in many classes, children routinely had the chance to make their own choices. Pairs and groups changed frequently in response to the ebb and flow of classroom activities and individual interests, so there was little danger of groupings – however composed – acquiring negative identities.

This collaborative approach was in marked contrast to the 'convenience groupings', most usually based on attainment, that, according to much prior research, characterize many primary children's classroom experience. A research review commissioned by the DfES (Kutnick *et al.* 2005) cites an observational study of 187 Year 2 and Year 5 classrooms (Kutnick *et al.* 2002) where it was rare to find any genuinely collaborative pair or small-group work. Only a small minority of teachers offered explicit support for the development of children's skills in learning together. Such convenience groupings, the authors comment, 'often limit the participation and understanding of children' (Kutnick *et al.* 2005: 40). These findings are echoed by those of another, more recent observational study of a class of children in their last two years of primary school (Bibby 2011). This study found that 'children were rarely given opportunities to collaborate, and we saw no evidence of their being supported to develop the skills required for collaboration to be productive' (2011: 112).

Wroxham teachers' commitment to encouraging learning together was both about developing forms of grouping that nurture positive learner identities and harnessing the power of the group to support and enhance everybody's participation and understanding. Organizing learning on a collaborative basis communicated to children that everybody was important, everybody had a place, everybody could learn from everybody else and could contribute to other people's learning. All the teachers expressed awareness of the negative messages that children almost inevitably drew from their experience of attainment-based grouping. After two years at the school, Sophie was convinced 'that it has a very negative effect' but wondered if she would ever have considered doing things differently if she had not come to Wroxham. 'I probably wouldn't have questioned the effect that it has on children's self-esteem and how valued they feel and how confident they feel.'

Cheryl was emphatic that she would never now go back to attainment-based grouping, 'I just think it's a horrible thing to do when you look back at it now.' She said she had seen many positive changes since she had introduced more flexible approaches. The children seemed to be more ready to turn to each other for help and work things out together; the 'I can't do it' attitude seemed to be a thing of the past. Children mixed more freely within the class generally and friendships had blossomed between children who would not have had much contact if grouping was organized according to notions of ability. She was often surprised by particular children who were quick to understand a new concept or felt ready to go and work independently. She noticed that she had come to expect more from all the children, now that she no longer planned with differentiated expectations for specific children in mind.

The conclusions that these two teachers had reached about attainment-based grouping were convincing, for them, because they had resulted from careful observation, development work and reflection on their experience over a period of time. No one told them what to do or how to do it. 'There's just a general expectation,' Sophie said, 'and the more that you work here, the more you understand it.' Their conclusions do, nevertheless, concur with consistent research findings about the effects of ability-based grouping, as summarized by Boaler (2009) in a powerful critique of the impact of this form of classroom organization on the teaching and learning of mathematics. Boaler argues, on the basis of a synthesis of research findings and her own professional experience, that 'The least helpful action that any school can take with a young learner of maths is to group them with other low achievers, give them lower level work, have low expectations for them, and communicate to them that they are of "low ability"' (2009: 98).

In elaborating her alternative pedagogy for mathematics, Boaler stresses, like the Wroxham teams, the importance of learning together. Children develop their mathematical thinking, she argues, by articulating their reasoning and explaining their ideas to one another. So activities need to be organized to maximize opportunities for interaction and discussion. A key condition for such discussion to be productive, though, is that young people be taught to work respectfully together, to value their different strengths, and to recognize what everybody gains when they help each other. Wroxham teachers were well aware of this need: there were ongoing discussions about how to choose a learning partner and how to *be* a good learning partner.

In Jo's class, children chose a learning partner at the start of each week, and sat with that partner for most activities. The children became familiar with the routine of choosing learning partners and were expected to prepare themselves by thinking in advance of two or three people they would like to work with, so that the process was accomplished quickly and smoothly. Names were written on lollysticks picked out at random; each child whose name was selected nominated a partner for that week until everyone was paired up. Jo spent time discussing with the children what makes a good learning partner, and why the best person was not always a close friend. The outcomes of these discussions were displayed on the classroom wall. She encouraged children to choose partners who would enable them to move out of their comfort zone. She also helped the children rehearse ways of refusing an invitation kindly, and reduced awkwardness to a minimum by making it clear that if a partnership was not working, there was always a way out. She found that other children were always ready to volunteer to change partners, in order to accommodate any difficulties arising. In keeping with the principle of choice, however, there was no coercion to work in pairs. Children could choose to work alone, for all or part of the week, if that was their preference.

Jo and her colleagues also spent time cultivating children's understanding of what they could contribute to each other's learning, stressing that it was perfectly legitimate to use other people's ideas, that the support children provided for one another could be as powerful as support from an adult. Children could learn from one another, even when partners differed in age, in confidence or in experience and skill as writers. For example, Simon and Martyn brought their Year 6 and Year 4 classes together to write play scripts collaboratively. They thought that collaboration across the two age groups could open up new learning opportunities for everybody. All the children could potentially benefit from working with different people with different experiences and interests. The disparity of ages and experience also offered the opportunity to bring about shifts in roles and patterns of engagement. Simon noted, for example, that when working collaboratively some children tended to sit back and allow others to do the thinking for them, or, alternatively, always played the dominant role. Mixing the year groups encouraged all the older children to become more active in their new role as more experienced writers, and more dominant younger children to engage with others' ideas more readily, when paired with older children.

Collaboration across the year groups also allowed the two teachers to model aspects of working together. At the start of the joint lesson, Simon and Martyn spent some considerable time exploring with children how to make a good choice of partner, what made a good partner, and modelling the process of editing text together. They talked about the qualities of a good 'critical friend', including being honest, supportive, patient, encouraging and maintaining focus. Then they modelled these qualities – and, humorously, their opposites – to bring the words to life for the children.

While the children were working on their writing, the teachers looked to see how effectively they were collaborating and displaying the qualities discussed, as well as providing any necessary input. Martyn was enthusiastic about what he saw: 'They were bouncing ideas off each other; they were supportive, weren't they? They were encouraging; they were very patient with each other; they were honest and they were clearly focused.' Martyn was impressed both with their serious engagement and with the quality of work that resulted. 'And they reflected on their writing,' he noted, 'they edited it, they improved it.'

We can see, then, that the teachers' commitment to encouraging learning together had social, emotional and intellectual dimensions. Overall, they were seeking to build communities of learners, within and between classes, increasingly able to draw on the resources of the group to support and empower one another's thinking and learning. This, they acknowledged, was work in progress; they all spoke of the challenges associated with enabling children to make good choices of learning partner and work effectively together. They drew attention to the tension between, on the one hand, their commitment to extending choice and enabling children to reflect on and learn from the choices they made; and on the other hand, intervening earlier in the process to enable children to make (as they thought) more productive choices. Simon, for example, described how he had wanted to intervene, during the play script activity, with two girls who always chose each other. They continued to choose each other, he felt, because they felt safe together – one more quiet and the other slightly more dominant – but he felt both would benefit from working with different people.

The teachers were also grappling with the tension between the many possible benefits of enabling children to choose their learning partner and the social and emotional pressures such choices created. Simon described how he attended to these pressures – the power of the glance, for example, as children caught each other's eye – and supported the children in rethinking their choices and groupings if not all children were included in a partnership or group. In their ongoing work to explore how best to build and strengthen collaborative working in their classrooms, the teachers supported each other and drew strength and inspiration from each other's ideas and support. Martyn acknowledged that he probably would not have persisted with learning partners if he had not been at Wroxham. But he had continued to explore ways to make the strategy work for his class, inspired by the strength and support of the collective: 'Because everyone does it and everyone's on the same wave length, you think it does work and it can work.'

Open-ended curriculum experiences

There was also an emerging agreement within the teaching teams about the importance of re-examining the curriculum from the children's perspective and trying to make learning more purposeful, worthwhile and rewarding from the children's point of view. They learned from experience how much more focused and engaged children were, and how the quality of their learning was enhanced, when tasks and activities connected to children's own interests and purposes, and when children were given space to explore ideas on their own terms. As we have seen, part of the rationale for increasing children's opportunities to make choices, to exercise control and to learn collaboratively was to make learning more interesting and personally meaningful to children. However, there was also a degree of consensus about the *kinds* of activities likely to enrich learning: for example, activities with authentic purposes and outcomes that mattered to the children; enquiry-based learning, led by the children's own questions and real-life problems; opportunities to learn from first-hand experiences; learning through imaginative play across the whole primary phase; hands-on experiences using real-world objects and artefacts; activities building on children's interests and sense of their own identities; activities inviting creativity and imagination, with scope for children to shape or direct their own learning; learning through genuine encounters with places and communities in the world outside school.

One multifaceted project, incorporating many of these elements, was carried out by Simon's Year 6 class, who designed, researched and led a series of activities for a class of younger children based at a local water mill and museum. The museum site had such a wealth of resources that it was decided the class should visit for a whole day, experience what was on offer in the morning, then meet with the museum staff in the afternoon to ask questions and plan a range of activities that could be led by the older children and taught to the class of 5- and 6-year-olds on a further day later in the year.

The children were very polite during the afternoon discussion but it was clear that what they really wanted to do was to touch the exhibits and take part in hands-on activities that were ostensibly for the younger children but in reality would excite them too. They pointed out that younger children would really love to use real water and soap to wash clothes with the Victorian washing dolly. Bread making would be an enjoyable activity but how about adding in all sorts of extra ingredients such as chocolate chips? The rhythm of the water mill inspired one child to suggest that they could bring percussion instruments from school so that a group could compose music to represent the mechanical sounds of the mill. Other children asked if they could handle Roman pottery and even bury it in the grounds so that others could excavate it. In the herb garden children could collect a sample of each herb and stick it to an identification card. The museum staff responded with enthusiasm to the children's ideas and agreed on a date in the summer term for a joint visit to be facilitated by the older children.

Science and history lessons back at school enabled Simon's class, in groups, to gain the background knowledge they needed to plan in detail the activities at the museum that they wished to provide for the younger children. Representatives from each planning group returned to the museum after school to liaise with the curator to ensure that their ideas were practicable and that the resources they hoped to use would be made available.

When the day for the joint visit finally arrived, the first group to arrive at the water mill were the 'teachers', Simon's class. The groups of children set about organizing their activities: each one would be run five times during the day, thereby enabling all 30 younger children to participate in groups of six. The younger class were accompanied by parents, with most groups having two adult helpers as well as a member of staff. The older children, however, took the lead in all aspects of the day, explaining the activities, allocating resources, managing behaviour and directing children to their next activity. One of the group leaders commented: 'It's harder for adults to think like (the younger children) but we're closer to them. . .we have to be very simple in our explanations.' Another reflected 'The big success is learning to do most of it themselves rather than them just watching us because that's what happens.' After the children had enjoyed their packed lunch, the older children organized parachute games. This careful thinking by the Year 6 teams about every small detail of the day ensured that there was no time at which children had nothing to do and could have become restless or difficult to manage. Consequently, the day was a huge success enjoyed by all who attended.

One child in Simon's class, interviewed after the museum day, commented: 'When I first went to Mill Green museum I thought that it would be a normal museum "listening and learning". When we started getting involved I found it fun and exciting, making bread and picking herbs that made me realize that "museum" didn't mean one type of place.' The museum staff were delighted with the highly organized and purposeful day and subsequently offered a family learning event one summer weekend with options inspired by the children's ideas. Many children from the school returned to the museum for that event as a way of sharing with their parents the experience of museum education that they had initiated.

In this project, the children's first-hand experience of the activities routinely on offer at the museum provided a springboard for them to generate their own ideas for activities that would be more hands-on and irresistibly engaging – for themselves as well as for younger children. During the period of the research, adjusting plans to incorporate more opportunities for learning through first-hand experience was a common theme among teachers' accounts of developments in their practice. For example, when staff were planning activities relating to a topic on Light and Dark, discussion led to the question 'How can children experience the dark?' In the summer term, young children awake to sunlight and go to bed before nightfall; it was therefore worthwhile to revisit the experience of darkness. The class teacher was planning to read the children *The Owl who was Afraid of the Dark*. Further discussion led to the idea that an enormous tree could be constructed in the classroom from cardboard and drapes. The tree trunk would be hollow and accessible via play tunnels borrowed from the nursery so that the interior of the tree could provide an exciting space for exploration with torches. The tree was built by a group of staff and the site manager after school.

First-hand experiences and imaginative play were also used as an inspiration for writing. Martyn, for example, talked to the headteacher about his concerns that some of the 8- and 9-year-olds in his class seemed reluctant to write. Their writing suggested that they were just going through the motions, with little personal investment in what they wrote. Following this conversation, Martyn went away to think about what might inspire them to write. Drawing on his own enthusiasm as a child for the story of Robin Hood, he came up with the idea of setting up a 'Robin Hood Day', to fire the children's imagination and involve them in some really engaging experiences to write about. When Robin Hood Day arrived, after excited planning discussions, including writing a typical menu for Robin Hood and his followers, the school skeleton, appropriately dressed, stood in for the Sheriff of Nottingham, and the children came in role as Merry Men and Women, equipped with bows and arrows. In the morning, they built dens and set up an archery range. They warmed bread and cooked over a small open fire. When they went back into school at the end of the day, the majority were so excited and motivated to write that they needed almost no support to get started. Martyn was delighted: 'I started to say "Well you might want to think about what you smelt, what you . . ." and I looked up and they were all busily writing!' Their motivation to write was inspired by more than just the fun that they had had during the day. Martyn realized that they were keen to write because they all had personal experiences to draw on. He was intrigued by how different each piece of writing was, because each child had selected different aspects of Robin Hood Day to write about.

The creative arts were also used as a way of stimulating imaginative thinking and inspiring writing. Visiting artists worked with groups of Year 6 children to create imaginary flying creatures, using willow and strong tissue paper soaked in paint and glue. The children constructed fabulous creatures with brightly coloured wings. These art workshops took place over two whole morning sessions, and became the inspiration for writing information leaflets as a guide to the wildlife in the skies of a fantasy rainforest. The workshops took place in February, at a time when staff in some primary schools were experiencing pressure to prepare for the SATs tests due to take place in May. Headteachers visiting the school commented on the bravery of allowing art to take place in Year 6 at that time of year.

Jo planned open-ended maths lessons with many possibilities for self-challenge. One such lesson was organized around work with 30 sets of dominoes. The children were invited to take part as mathematicians and 'to have fun with other mathematicians'. A series of activities was offered, all of which required the children to investigate patterns, hypothesize, test ideas and explore combinations of numbers. Activities included variations on the traditional game of dominoes, for example arranging touching dominoes to make a specific number, using addition and subtraction; making small chains of dominoes where touching numbers are alternately odd and even; and creating magic squares where the lines of dominoes all add up to the same number. The tasks were progressively challenging, building on children's previous experiences of problem-solving activities. The resources were unusual and attractive and the mathematical activities ensured that all children could keep encountering new ideas, developing their thinking at their own pace with appropriate scaffolding from the resources or an adult. However, each child could choose an entry point to access the activity, ensuring sufficient challenge for all. These lessons, and others like them, embodied the message that learning is endlessly enticing: no one can ever finish learning.

Simon took the decision to celebrate learning with his Year 6 children by organizing a visit to the Natural History Museum in London on the day before the SATs tests. Simon had no use for prepared worksheets. He talked with the children about what was available and allowed them to choose where to go and how to spend the time based on their personal interests. He also booked the children into the Discovery Centre where they were able to explore rarely available resources such as snake skins and crocodile teeth. He talked enthusiastically about all the different activities available to children, and the scope for them to pursue their own enquiries. 'The people there are facilitators. They don't teach them; they follow the child's interest. So the child might pick up a beetle and put it under the microscope and then they sketch it and find out if it's similar to another beetle.' They might then go on to identify different body parts and find out about their functions in the living animal. Even though it was an ordinary school day, the museum was deserted, presumably because staff in many schools were using the day for last minute revision in preparation for the tests in the coming week. Simon's rationale was that the children needed to be reminded why learning is fascinating, instead of being reminded how to perform in test situations.

Access to these kinds of rich learning experiences across all areas of the curriculum enabled children and adults to appreciate what becomes possible when a group of learners are free to explore ideas and different ways of working together. All these activities were carefully planned, but learning outcomes were not specified in advance: there was no need to do so. When children are engaged in purposeful, challenging, open-ended activities such as these, it is unnecessary – indeed impossible – to define in advance what they will learn as they explore, enquire and experiment. The experiences we have described were not only genuinely open-ended, they were also accessible to all children; everybody could take part. Furthermore, the teachers trusted that the exploration and collaborative working that they had built into these experiences would result in worthwhile learning for everybody.

Involving children in assessing their own learning

As we saw in Chapter 2, quite early in the period after Alison joined the school, the decision was taken to involve children more actively in the assessment of their own learning. Learning review meetings were set up during the autumn and spring terms, at which children talked with their class teacher and parents about their learning; they were also given the responsibility of writing their own reports in the form of a dialogue with their teachers. During the period of the research, members of the teaching team also began to give more concentrated thought to involving children in assessing their own learning on a day-by-day basis. Self-assessment was another important way of encouraging children's active involvement in and control over their learning: encouraging them to monitor and reflect on their own thinking and understanding, to engage in dialogue with their teacher and with peers about their learning and share responsibility for deciding how to move forward.

In their seminal paper, *Inside the Black Box,* Black and Wiliam (1998) present the research base for their claim that formative assessment, including self-assessment, has a key role to play in enhancing learning and enabling young people to become better learners. They suggest that, as a starting point for improving formative assessment, teachers should be asking themselves the question 'Do I really know enough about the understanding of my pupils to be able to help each of them?' (1998: 13). At Wroxham, teachers began to explore ways to find out more about their children's thinking and understanding, including experimenting with the use of journals and self-assessment sheets to enable children to reflect on their learning at the end of particular activities.

In Simon's Year 6 class, for example, the children asked for small booklets with blank pages that they could use for drawing if they chose. In science, these booklets were used to record learning at the end of a topic. So, after a sustained study of habitats and adaptation, Simon asked the children to explain, through drawings, captions or extended text, what they understood about the ways in which a particular animal was adapted to a particular habitat. For maths, the children recorded ideas and explanations relating to whatever topic they had been learning during the course of a week. The books were also used to track progress and recognize achievement. In English, children chose pieces of their own work they were proud of and stuck them in their books. Simon wanted them to recognize and celebrate their progress, as well as deciding on and recording the next steps.

Jo, the Year 5 teacher, used self-assessment journals in order to encourage an ongoing dialogue about learning with each child. The dialogue could also be about emotional issues that children wanted to share with her in confidence. At the end of an activity, such as writing a story, she would ask the children to jot down what they felt that they had learned about story writing. Jo then responded to each child's comment. It gradually became clear, however, that in order for children to play a full part in these various initiatives and for self-assessment to become meaningful and integral to their learning rather than tokenistic, children needed to be helped to develop a language in which to formulate their thoughts and engage in dialogue about learning with their teacher and peers.

Jo chose this as the topic for her small-scale research project, while study-ing for her master's degree (Smith 2007). She reasoned that developing a shared meta-language for talking about learning and assessment would enable her to communicate more effectively with the young people in her class about their learning. At the start of the research, children tended to use smiley or sad faces to indicate how they felt about their learning, but what the children were expressing through these drawings was open to many interpretations.

To extend their capacity to express their thoughts about their learning, she involved the children as co-researchers in observing and recording what teacher and children actually said during their own class circle time, when they talked about learning. The children helped to tally instances of particular words and phrases and discarded expressions to do with classroom routines that they judged not to be learning-related. They explored meanings in more depth by trying to match up things Jo said with things they said themselves, in order to see if they all meant the same thing. They chose to categorize the learning-related language in terms of de Bono's thinking hats (de Bono 2000). The six thinking hats were a popular feature of Jo's interactive classroom display on 'Learning Tools', prompting children to adopt a variety of different thinking strategies to assist their learning. Moving into another medium of expression, the children drew and painted metaphorical pictures representing their feelings about learning, showing themselves, for example, 'stuck' in a swamp and 'lost' in a jungle when confronted by challenges; or alternatively 'walking on a rainbow' when they had done their best and been successful.

Following these activities, Jo began to notice changes in the children's attitudes to learning and in their self- and peer assessments. Children expressed greater confidence in their learning and their capacity to improve their own work by reflecting on it. They were more ready to accept mistakes and difficul-ties as part of learning. They began to write in a more elaborated way in their self-assessment journals, and to approach the task of writing as a genuine act of communication. They made more active use of thinking tools, ideas and strategies, as a result of having talked about them together. There was evidence that a shared understanding of the purpose of self-assessment was developing. Jo commented: 'All the children seemed to understand that if you write a comment about your learning, your teacher will value it and respond to it.' In circle time, Hassan expressed his understanding of the reciprocal relationship involved when he said to Jo: 'When I do my comments, it sort of helps you to do the plan for the next day because you know what we got stuck on so you can do something for that.'

Handing over a significant degree of control to young people and working in partnership with them, rather than taking the lead in directing everything, were the key conditions in making all these developments possible. Jo wrote in her thesis: 'At the heart of formative assessment is the shift from the teacher as the giver of knowledge to someone who facilitates learning and is led by the learners' (p. 18). She represented the development of her thinking through the project in Figure 3.1. This expresses her understanding of the critical role that a shared language for learning plays in enabling the interplay between all the other important conditions (including choice and control) that *together* support children in becoming effective learners.

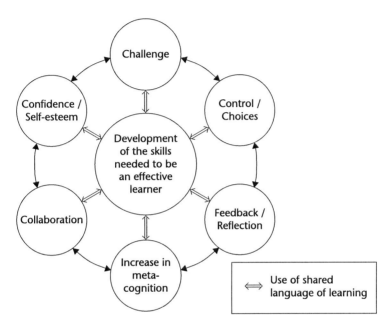

Figure 3.1   The role of a shared language for learning

Source: Smith (2007).

Extending freedom to learn

As we have examined the common elements of pedagogy that the teaching teams at Wroxham chose to focus on, in developing their practices during the period of the research, it has become apparent that these elements are not independent, separate parts of their repertoire. Rather, they are interdependent, interlocking means of achieving a single core purpose: enabling children to experience greater freedom and control over their learning. The teaching teams sought to increase the spaces and opportunities for children to formulate and pursue their own ideas and questions and to exercise control in as many areas of classroom life as possible; they believed (a belief increasingly confirmed by their experience) that in doing so they were creating conditions for the children to become more active, powerful and committed learners. Though they did not use the term, they could be seen as acting in the spirit of 'transformability': the belief that there is always the potential for children to become better learners, and that teachers can be instrumental in enabling positive changes to happen in the future through the decisions they make in the present. Similarly, though few of them used the language of 'limits', sometimes when they articulated their reasons for introducing or developing particular practices, it was clear that they were drawing on their knowledge and understanding of some of the external conditions and internal states of mind that can inhibit or reduce young people's capacity to learn.

When we probe the thinking underlying the development of these elements of pedagogy, we can see that the principles guiding teachers' decision-making closely mirror the three core principles – 'co-agency', 'trust' and 'everybody' – that inspired Alison's vision for school development. Their choices increasingly reflected a view of learning as a partnership between teacher and children (co-agency). They were informed by a belief that children do want to learn, that they can and will be infinitely resourceful given the opportunity (trust). They embodied commitment to every child's learning, by increasing space and flexibility to cater for diverse interests and needs, by ensuring that doors were always kept open and that there was always the potential for all children to experience achievement (everybody).

We can see, then, that the ideas underlying these developments are closely aligned with Alison's vision for the school. It is not difficult to make links between the emerging common focus on extending freedom to learn and the foundations laid by new structures and initiatives described in Chapter 2. Ideas about the importance of listening to children, for example, and giving them more say in and control over their learning, embodied in circle group meetings and learning review meetings, have become essential tenets in people's thinking and decision making, increasingly pervading all areas of classroom learning. Nevertheless, the teachers were adamant that developments were in no sense imposed. They each felt free and in control of their own learning; they each developed their practices in their own ways and in their own time. The freedom to learn that they were focusing upon creating in their classrooms for their learners was also extended to them as the context and condition for their own professional learning. Consensus around priority areas for the development of practice came about through a growing intermeshing of teachers' own purposes, values and principles, with those that Alison was seeking to foster at a collective level.

We can follow how this process occurred most clearly in the experience of teachers who were new to the school at the start of the research. New teachers said that they were not pressurized to adopt any particular strategies or ways of thinking. They observed what others were already doing and made their own decisions to try things out. They began to evolve new practices in ways that made sense to them and, learning from their experience, gradually began to extend the range of opportunities that they offered. Their understanding of the purposes underlying these new practices and the alignment of their own values with them was a gradual, unfolding experience. Their commitment grew as they saw for themselves the positive impact on children; this in turn led them to rethink and rearticulate their sense of what was possible, what they therefore wanted for their children and their growing sense of power to make it happen. All this thinking they were doing for themselves. And because they felt free and in charge of the process, they also felt able to resist and contest ideas and practices that appeared to be in conflict with their own current perceptions and values. While they were obviously aware of the collective flow inspiring them to move in a particular direction, they were determined – and were encouraged – at each stage to think things through for themselves and arrive at their own conclusions.

4   Rethinking learning relationships

The focus on extending freedom to learn that inspired the work of the staff group collectively during the period of the research involved more than the development and refinement of new practices. It also involved work to develop the kinds of relationships needed to sustain and foster increased freedom to learn. These were not just pedagogic relationships but also ways of being, relating and working together that increasingly permeated every aspect of the life of the community. These developments did not just happen but required systematic effort, insight, compassion and risk taking. In this chapter, we draw on a series of examples to explore the nature of these relationships and what was involved, practically, in negotiating and developing them. What were staff doing to build the kinds of relationships they felt were needed as the bedrock of their work in school? What common themes can be discerned among the group as a whole? How were these themes reflected in people's actions at particular moments? What challenges did people experience in attempting to enact these kinds of enabling relationships? What links can we ascertain between this work around relationships and the *Learning without Limits* principles that informed the headteacher's vision for the overall development of the school?

Challenge, congruence and the 'natural balance'

One powerful source of insight into the distinctive characteristics of relationships that were being fostered within the community as a whole is provided by one teacher's eventually successful struggle with a challenging class over the course of her second year of teaching. Sophie joined the staff at Wroxham as a newly qualified teacher in September 2005. During her first term, she was struck by the contrast between the ideas and practices that she encountered at the school and those to which she had been introduced on her initial teaching course. During this time, it was in her words 'very much teach the curriculum, this is what you have got to get through. The approach here is quite different. It's a lot of hands-on activities, a lot of role play, and it's letting the children explore different avenues and things that interest them.' This approach made perfect sense to her, so, although no one put any pressure on her to do so, she began to introduce some changes into her teaching, trying out for herself ways of giving children more freedom and control, offering them more choices in their learning, giving them space to pursue their own interests and using more hands-on activities and role play.

It took a while, she recalled, during that first year, to develop the confidence and skills to work so differently from the approaches recommended to her during her course, but she was excited by how the children responded. As well as making 'fantastic' progress, Sophie was struck by their enthusiasm and the 'spark' that they displayed in their learning. By the end of her first year, she was convinced that 'the Wroxham strategies', as she called them, really worked and was looking forward to using and building on her new repertoire with her next class of 6- and 7-year-olds. However, this class presented a whole new set of challenges and Sophie quickly realized that she would not be able to work with them as she had done with the previous group. 'Within a few weeks they started to say to me, "We're the bad class, people don't like us. No one wants to work with us."' She was shocked that children so young should have picked up such negative messages. She was taken aback that they seemed to find it difficult to stay on a chair, sit at a table or keep focused on the tasks in hand, and was worried that this was affecting the quality of their work. She found that she was responding to them in ways that made her feel uncomfortable. She knew that she did not want to spend 'a whole year going in and being hard and negative. That's how they made you feel.' She understood that this was not the kind of person she wanted to be nor the kind of relationship she wanted to have with the children. Nor did she want to be yet another person, in the children's eyes, who saw them negatively.

So she decided she must find another way, one that was congruent with the new emphasis in her practice on extending freedom to learn and with the kind of teacher that she aspired to be. Her alternative way was to try to work *with* the children rather than against them, involving them at each stage in working out positive strategies to make their classroom experience more harmonious and purposeful. After listening and acknowledging the children's sense of hurt and rejection about being 'the bad class', Sophie shifted the discussion onto more positive territory by asking the children what they would like other people to say about them. Together, they constructed a list of positive words, and this became a shared point of reference within the group. They now had a collective sense of 'how we want to be, and be seen by others', and this was used by staff and children to recognize and affirm positive contributions to the well-being and harmony of the group. The children also identified some collective goals for themselves, such as better listening, which were displayed on large posters in the classroom. At their suggestion, ticks were added alongside the goals each time these were successfully met. Once the original goals became accepted group norms, new goals were discussed and agreed upon.

To build on their interests and create a stronger sense of investment in classroom learning, Sophie also began to involve the children more fully in planning curriculum activities and experiences, first relating to work on the Victorians in the autumn term and then, in the spring term, the Roald Dahl project described in some detail in Chapter 3. It was with this project that Sophie felt things had really turned a corner. The children's attitude to their learning completely changed. Asked why she felt that had happened, she explained, 'It's about giving them the power back, finding those key things that capture their imagination, providing them with opportunities to learn about things that excite them.' Involving the children in this way sent many important messages to them about how they were seen, valued and trusted, showing that their thinking – not just the teacher's – really counted.

Sophie made time to reflect with the children constantly 'on every little thing, thinking, well, that didn't work, why didn't it work, or that worked really well, why did it work?' Dialogue was critically important at every stage. She tried to be very careful that the children saw her as 'part of it, rather than the director'. The process had to be genuinely two-way, with trust and respect on both sides. Sophie did not want the children simply to be modifying their behaviour for *her* but for themselves. She wanted them to appreciate for themselves that this was a better way of being together, so that they would take these understandings with them when they moved to the next class.

It was not always plain sailing, however. There was a crisis point early in the spring term when a distressed child lashed out and hurt Sophie. It brought her close to breaking point herself. Alison and Jo, her mentor, provided vital support, helping her to recognize the huge distance that she and the class had already travelled together. The confidence and reassurance of colleagues helped her to maintain her conviction that the direction she and the class had taken together was the right one. Eventually, not very long after this event, things did indeed fall into place. As Sophie described it, looking back, she and the class 'just found a natural balance, a natural way of working'. This 'natural balance' is arguably the antithesis of some behaviour management programmes where power rests firmly with the teacher and compliance is the goal rather than the development of children's capacity for autonomous judgement. In Sophie's class, it was arrived at through a genuinely open, two-way process ('you adjust to them and they adjust to you') and was the product of everything they had done together, Sophie insisted, the mistakes as well as the successes. It was unique to the history and experience of her work with that particular class.

Despite the unique nature of the resulting relationship, however, Sophie's approach does capture some of the key characteristics of work to develop relationships congruent with the aim of extending freedom to learn within the learning community more generally. First, she incorporated work to enhance meaning and communication between herself and the children by extending common ground and *building shared understandings* between herself and the children, and between the children themselves. Secondly, she sought to liberate children from dependence upon her own adult approval, replacing approval with *acceptance* and autonomy. Thirdly, she made active and constant use of *empathy*, determined continually to see the world through the eyes of the other, acknowledging the power of emotions in learning. And fourthly, she maintained *steadfastness of purpose*, even in the most challenging situations. In the rest of this chapter, we examine each of these key characteristics in turn. We analyse other examples of work in the area of relationships, documented during the period of the research, and consider how these were helping to promote and sustain freedom to learn. We explore how these common areas of work were also necessary building blocks in the creation of a school guided by *Learning without Limits* principles.

Towards shared understandings

In the example we have examined in detail, Sophie's work to build shared understandings focused on what it means to participate as a positive member of a harmonious learning collective. The 'natural balance' was in part an indication that enough common ground had been established between adults and children and between the children themselves for classroom life to operate smoothly. The shared understandings achieved through ongoing dialogue created a secure framework in which people could act autonomously; they knew and understood the expectations because they had created them together; they knew what was possible and where the limits lay and could make their choices accordingly.

In other classes, a central focus of ongoing dialogue was around the nature of learning and what it means to be a good learner. Simon, the Year 6 teacher, was convinced that 'teaching is all about relationships'; through his relationships with his class he set out to enable them to build what Dweck and Leggett (1988) call a 'mastery' orientation: the belief that however challenging children are finding it to learn something, they will get there in the end with persistent effort. Dweck and her colleagues contrast this positive way of thinking with a 'helpless' orientation, where children respond to failure as a sign that they lack the intelligence needed to be successful and that there is nothing they can do to help themselves. ' "Can't" is banned in my class,' Simon told us, ' "Can't do it *yet*" is one of the first things I say to them.' Simon openly talked with his class about his own learning, encouraging them to see learning as a never-ending process. Through his reflections on his own learning, he encouraged them towards a view of a good learner as someone who was willing 'to have a go', to make brave attempts at trying out new ideas, to accept mistakes as a necessary and inevitable part of learning, and to do all these things because of their understanding of what good learning entails, rather than to gain the approval of their teacher. He, in turn, sought to reach every child by knowing them individually, never giving up, seeking to 'open everything up', to find a way forward together.

The Year 5 teacher, Jo, also regarded ongoing dialogue with the children in her class about learning and how to be a good learner as a key element of her practice. In Chapter 3, we saw how Jo, like other teachers, worked with the children to develop a shared understanding of the value of learning with a partner, choosing and being a good learning partner. We also saw how she recognized the need for children's self-assessments to be supported by the development of a shared language if they were to move beyond drawing smiley or sad faces to represent their thoughts and evaluations. Jo's research into the language of learning and formative assessment in her classroom involved the children as student researchers. For Jo it would have seemed unnatural to conduct classroom research without sharing both process and outcomes with the children, whom she described as a 'community of learners'. Her enquiry was genuinely open-ended. For example, introducing a class discussion about words they might use to describe learning in their self-assessment, she explained: 'I don't know, so you can't be wrong. It is all new to me too.' The children were not inducted into Jo's ready-made ways of thinking, but were engaged in a genuine learning experience. As the year progressed, both Jo and the children gained in confidence and developed a shared understanding of self-assessment and its purposes.

Building shared understandings about learning, about how to be a good learner, about strategies that good learners use, played a significant role, for these teachers, in enabling children to take up and use fully the freedoms extended to them. In an environment designed to foster active learning, children's willingness to make good use of the opportunities provided was clearly going to be importantly affected by how they construed learning, by how they made sense of and responded to challenges, and their expectations of success. Setting aside ability-based practices was not necessarily sufficient in itself to change ingrained self-perceptions and attitudes, especially among older children. Bringing parents in on the discussions about learners and learning was also an important part of the process. Mindful that the children's ideas were deeply influenced by their parents' beliefs and experiences, members of the teaching team, in partnership with children, sought imaginative ways to involve parents and build shared understandings about the values underpinning developments taking place in the school. For example, the children in Jo's class, fired up by their involvement in her research, came up with the idea of organizing a 'Bring your parent to school' event. The idea of inviting parents to experience what learning was like in school generated enthusiastic discussion about how this might be organized, who could be invited and what activities might be offered. The children decided that they themselves would take on the role of teaching the adults, and a debate ensued about what they wanted their parents to understand about learning. Invitations were sent home and responses were eagerly awaited.

Parents, grandparents or older siblings from over half the class arrived in school several weeks later. Apprehension among some adults about returning to school as a pupil rapidly evaporated as the programme for the morning was explained by the children. A balance of theory and practice had been planned so that the adults would understand why they were being asked to work in particular ways. The class had collaboratively developed a 'learning toolbox' display which provided a range of strategies such as 'how to get unstuck when you are confused'. Activities planned for the morning included an explanation of thinking hats (de Bono 2000), team building skills, outdoor learning and composing music. Adults and children took part in a carousel of activities both within and beyond the classroom, including collecting and identifying insects outside in the grounds. The children worked in partnership with their class teacher to identify activities that they believed would help their parents understand the learning that they valued themselves. Practices such as teamwork, sharing one's thinking with a learning partner, problem solving and learning from mistakes within a collaborative community were illustrated very effectively by the events of the morning. The children were clear that these were the aspects of learning that enabled them to embrace challenge within their everyday tasks.

Building and communicating acceptance

There was evidence, too, that teachers felt it important to move away from relationships based on approval, in order to support and foster increased freedom to learn. As we saw earlier, Sophie was keen to develop a way of working with her challenging class that did not involve clamping down or enforcing unthinking compliance. She knew that she did not want children to modify their behaviour just in order to gain her approval; she knew that she wanted the children to find ways of being and learning together that were personally and collectively satisfying – the 'natural balance'.

In her research with her class around the language of assessment, Jo observed that some of their comments seemed to suggest that they were doing it *for her*, rather than because they actually understood how self-assessment could contribute to their learning. She realized that there was further work to be done to help them to take the next step, to recognize the value of self-assessment as an integral part of what a good learner does. In the conclusion to her thesis, she recorded this as a priority area to work on with her class (Smith 2007: 62). Similarly, in Simon's and Jo's accounts of how they worked on the concept of 'learning' with their classes, we saw that both were committed to helping children to formulate and be guided by their own sense of what it is to be a good learner, rather than simply taking on board and complying with the teacher's definition. Both were aware of the danger that learning to please the teacher could rule out the possibility of other more worthwhile kinds of learning.

Like Sophie, both Simon and Jo understood that their aim of extending freedom to learn in their classrooms implied the need for a different kind of relationship with their children. They wanted to release children from the burden of trying to guess what they needed to do or say in order to win their teacher's praise, to give them freedom to think for themselves, safe in the knowledge that they were accepted, trusted and valued for who they were, as unique individual people, rather than for the extent to which they measured up to what (they thought) their teacher wanted.

Carl Rogers (1969, 1983) calls this kind of relationship 'acceptance'. Acceptance, in Rogers's terms, is not simply about recognizing and valuing individuals as they are; it is profoundly transformative. It is the necessary condition for autonomous learning, the means by which the educator creates the conditions of psychological safety without which learning is inevitably inhibited. At Wroxham, the teachers' view of 'acceptance' seemed to be centrally concerned with trust: trust in children's desire to learn, trust in their powers as learners, trust in their ability to work sensitively and productively together, trust in their infinite resourcefulness to use learning opportunities in countless unpredictable ways. Most importantly, it involved communicating to children that they had, and *could not lose*, these kinds of trust, so they need not be preoccupied with trying to win their teacher's approval. They could put their effort into asking their own questions, thinking things out for themselves and pursuing their own lines of inquiry, without being afraid of making mistakes or failing to reach a required standard.

From our study of the common elements of pedagogy in Chapter 3, it is clear that the existence of authentic trust, in these various forms, did not come about simply through an act of will. It came about gradually and became more securely established as staff tried out practices designed to give children more autonomy and were impressed by how effectively and creatively the children made use of them. For Sophie, the choice of an approach based on trust, in preference to imposing her authority on the class, was risky indeed. She did not know in advance that trust in such young children would turn out to be well founded. But once she and the class had worked through their difficulties, and she knew from her own experience that the trust had been well placed, this gave her solid ground from which to extend her trust to the next class with confidence.

It seemed that the more trust that was invested in children, the more competent and resourceful they showed themselves to be. For example, a local secondary headteacher who had heard about the weekly circle group meetings at Wroxham asked Alison to address a senior leaders' staff meeting on the subject of pupil voice. Alison discussed this with Jo and they decided to invite the Year 5 children to plan and deliver a presentation about their learning themselves. The children were asked if they would like to participate and a small group volunteered to prepare a PowerPoint presentation. The presentation was written entirely by the children and was completely child-led. When the children arrived with staff at the school to make their presentation, they were directed to a tiered lecture theatre. Despite this daunting venue, the children spoke with clarity and passion about the choices they were offered in their learning, the exciting opportunities that they experienced in school and the importance of listening to all members of the school community. Not only did the children present their ideas clearly and with humour as a group, they also responded with enthusiasm and thoughtfulness to a wide range of questions from secondary colleagues. Their response to the demands of the event richly confirmed their teachers' trust in their capacity to rise to challenges and to communicate their thinking confidently when they themselves were in control.

The shift from approval to trust-based acceptance as the foundation for relationships was significantly assisted, across the teaching team as a whole, by the gradual elimination of the vocabulary of differential ability. Trust, as reflected in the Wroxham teachers' thinking and practice, is arguably the antithesis of the differential expectations set up by ability-based thinking, where high expectations are by definition reserved for the few children deemed most capable. As the teachers explored alternatives to ability grouping and noticed how the children responded, they not only revised their expectations but progressively ceased to have recourse to ability categories as tools to support them in planning and talking about children. The absence of hierarchical grouping, with all its potentially negative messages, and the absence of labels pinning children down to specific, stable identities, created conditions in which trust in every child's capacity to learn could be authentically created and communicated, so that all children could be free to learn and accepted as themselves.

In Chapter 3, we examined some of the positive changes that Cheryl noticed in her Year 1 class when she replaced ability grouping with a more flexible approach. Mark, a child in her class who flourished in this new climate, was absolutely fascinated by the natural world. He was extremely knowledgeable about animals and talked confidently about what he had learned from his family, from using books, watching television and exploring the internet. However, he found writing very difficult; there was a mismatch between what he could express in spoken language and his limited skill in producing written text, but because his class teacher, Cheryl, no longer used ability groups and

had begun to offer more choices to the children, he did not suffer the humili-
ation of being labelled a non-writer. He was observed poring over a book about
caterpillars: he recorded his learning through careful, detailed drawings, which
he then labelled. His friend Arun helped him to find the key words he needed
and even showed him how to form some of his letters. When he was invited to
share his work, Mark offered to tell the rest of the class what he had learned
about caterpillars from the detailed illustrations in the book. His general
knowledge and enthusiasm for sharing interesting information were admired
by his classmates and by his teacher; his difficulties with learning to write did
not become a defining label.

Parents who were interviewed during the period of the research had a clear
understanding of why staff at the school chose on principle to avoid labelling
and grouping children by ability, and for the most part they were strongly in
sympathy with the underlying reasoning. One parent explained '. . . putting
children in certain groups and telling them you are the bright ones and you're
the dumb ones doesn't work in many ways. It doesn't work for parents: you get
the competition "Oh my child's in such and such a group", "Oh my child is
not".' Most parents saw the policy as beneficial both for their own children
and for children in general. They were aware of how sensitive children were to
the effects of ability labelling and grouping, which one parent described as
'unhealthy'. Another, who thought her son would have been in the top group,
feared that this could have led him to become arrogant. A third, who thought
her daughter might have been placed in a bottom group because of spelling
difficulties, said that this could have led to her feeling demoralized and demo-
tivated, permanently accepting failure. The effects of ability labelling, one
parent said, could last a lifetime. They agreed that every child needs encouragement and stimulation; children should be encouraged to feel that 'anything
and everything is possible', to approach learning confidently and to seize every
opportunity to have a go. Establishing this confidence was the primary goal,
the parents said, and once established, academic success would follow.

So how was children's confidence built up? The parents agreed that the
absence of ability labelling was crucial. One parent explicitly used the language
of 'freedom', saying that without ability-based comparisons 'everyone feels
free to learn'. Confidence grows because everyone 'feels equal' and 'feels important', not least because there were so many opportunities for children to
express their thoughts and feelings about their learning, to experience being
listened to and to see their ideas not only being heard but acted upon. They
agreed that 'everyone has their say', and everyone is treated as an individual
with a unique contribution to make.

The few doubts that were expressed were about practical strategies, for
example whether encouraging children to choose their own level of work
would provide sufficient challenge for all children. One parent was concerned
that her son might not be sufficiently motivated to choose the most

challenging work, even if he was capable of it. Another considered that Wroxham's approach created more pressures for teachers. Other parents noted that they had had doubts at first, but had been won over by seeing that their children were thriving. The parent who had been concerned that her son would go for the easy options was reassured to see that his teacher took active steps to challenge him. Her second child, who had struggled with writing initially, had also clearly benefited from her teacher's careful support and encouragement so that she faced 'just enough' challenge.

It would be misleading, though, to imply that shifting from approval to acceptance as the basis for relationships was without its problems either for adults or for children, as the following incident illustrates. Derek, the author of the 'famous' notebooks described in Chapter 3, was not only passionate about learning; he also had a very short temper. Although he tried to solve any friendship difficulties with words rather than with his fists, he was quick to take offence. Any implied or actual criticism could cause him to fly into a rage and storm out of the classroom and hide.

One afternoon Derek burst out of the classroom shouting a variety of expletives and locked himself in the lavatory, refusing to come out. When the deputy head, Simon, finally succeeded in encouraging Derek to unlock the door, he calmly asked the boy to write down what had happened. Derek's class was being taught by Mrs N, standing in for his class teacher, Jo, that afternoon. His list of complaints is reproduced below:

> **Complaints about Mrs N**
> I want Mrs N to use a nice and sensible tone of voice.
> I want Mrs N not to teach me ever again.
> I want Mrs N not to rush me on my work.
> I want Mrs N to be a good teacher for once.
> I want Mrs N to think about others more carefully.
> I want Mrs N to realize that small children do get upset very easily.

Once he had written down his thoughts Derek felt able to return to class and apologize. The following day, the headteacher sat down with Derek to talk about what had happened. She listened to his list of complaints and asked what had made him so angry. He replied indignantly that it had been almost the end of the afternoon, he had finished his work and the teacher had then instructed him to copy out the recipe that they would be using when they made bread the following week. Derek complained that this was a waste of time but she insisted. It was this insistence that had triggered his outburst. Alison explained why such an extreme reaction was unacceptable; now in a calmer frame of mind, Derek could articulate very clearly why he should not have lost his temper. However, he still insisted that he had been right and that the teacher should not have asked him to do something that he considered to be a waste of time.

As a beneficiary of the staff's commitment to nurturing autonomy rather than compliance, Derek arguably did have a legitimate grievance. He did not feel that he had been treated kindly or fairly, nor had he been listened to and trusted, by Mrs N, as the active, committed learner that he knew himself to be. Instead of bowing down compliantly, he had stood up for his right as a learner to spend his time on worthwhile tasks. In his eyes, it was the teacher who had broken the contract, though he recognized his own fault in giving such vociferous expression to his anger.

The situation required careful handling. It was important to ensure that Derek knew his point of view had been taken seriously, while also helping him learn from the incident in a dignified and creative way. Alison suggested that he might like to plan and teach his own class a lesson the following week. This, she thought, might help him to gain an insight into relationships between teachers and children from a different perspective. The idea was not as risky as it might appear, as she knew that the class teacher, Jo, would support the idea and help Derek, ensuring that he was able to lead the class effectively. She also knew Derek well and judged that he would be capable of carrying out a teaching role. She offered to talk with Jo, and see what could be arranged. Derek enthusiastically agreed and suggested that he teach a poetry lesson.

Although a week passed between the classroom incident and the planned lesson there was never any doubt on anyone's part that time would be made for Derek's lesson to take place, or that he would have the courage to proceed with the idea. Derek planned the poetry lesson using the school's lesson plan format and prepared all the resources he needed, with Jo's support. Alison joined the lesson and wrote a poem as instructed by Derek, now very much the teacher. She let him know that she had finished early and needed something else to do and he asked her to write another poem, which she agreed to do. After the lesson, no one felt the need to debrief Derek about what it had felt like to take the lead. They trusted Derek to learn from the experience and his subsequent behaviour showed that he had indeed done so.

Derek continued to be a strong presence within his class; on many occasions he was difficult to work with. With his quick temper, Derek's relationships with his teachers and peers could easily have become, and remained, adversarial. Instead, by listening to him and showing him respect as a learner, and by treating lapses of temper as opportunities for learning, the staff enabled his genuine passion for learning to flourish. In an interview with other children towards the end of Year 6, Derek's contributions suggest that he was well aware of the significance of the freedom he had been given:

> Derek: I think . . . the child needs freedom in their school, they need to make their own choices, if they're not allowed to do that, I don't know . . .

Alison: They rebel?

Derek: Yeah, because if they're not getting their way, they make their own way.

The importance of empathy

For the Wroxham teachers, 'acceptance' did not just mean trust. It also implied empathy with children's feelings and perspectives, a persistent effort on teachers' part to step outside their own frames of reference to try to make sense of the children's worlds, their experiences of the classroom, their thinking and learning, from their point of view. We have already seen how Sophie's capacity to communicate empathy was an important aspect of her work with her class. Her genuine understanding of the children's feelings, her ability to place herself in their shoes and think about things from their perspective enabled them to feel that she was working *with* them to find better ways of being together in the classroom. For Jo, too, empathy was central to her relationship with her class. She told us how she had learned from her children the importance of treating their work as a gift, of responding to it with as much awareness and care for the feelings of the giver as she would a gift, and also to give something of herself in return.

Teachers' empathy for children's feelings and perspectives made space for children to create their own conditions for learning, free from unnecessary restrictions. When a senior inspector (HMI) spent a day at the school, on an official visit, her parting comment was that she would never forget a moment in a Year 1 classroom, when, among a group of children busily writing, she had observed a boy dressed from head to toe as a tiger. It is interesting to reflect on why this observation made such an impression on an experienced professional. Perhaps she realized that, at Wroxham, wearing a tiger suit while writing was not a remarkable event. She saw for herself that there was no queue of children clamouring for their turn to wear the suit; there were no adults hovering to ensure that everyone was concentrating on the task in hand. Daniel simply sat down to write wearing a tiger suit, and that was that. The inspector probably knew that, in many schools, the prevailing adult view would be that tiger suits and writing do not go together. At Wroxham, people understood that, in the child's world, there is no discontinuity between wearing a tiger suit and writing. On the contrary, inside a tiger suit may be exactly the right place for writing, a place where the imagination can run free, and where a child can feel relaxed, warm and safe, ready to confront the challenge of writing a story.

For Darrelle, the Year 3 teacher, relationships based on empathy were the necessary corollary of what she referred to as her 'child-centred' approach. Darrelle's sense of the importance of empathy had strong roots in her own experience at school. She knew what it felt like to be a child who was seemingly not noticed or valued until one day she scored highly in a mock O Level exam. Her teacher, who 'had not spoken to me in two whole years' suddenly started saying 'Well, let's ask Darrelle this.' She had become worthy of notice and attention only once she had demonstrated outstanding attainment. Darrelle had also never forgotten a child she met on teaching practice, who had repeatedly come into conflict with his class teacher. The child confided that 'she thinks I'm nothing, she treats me like dirt' and for him this meant the complete breakdown of the relationship: 'If she thinks I'm nothing she's nothing to me.' Darrelle was deeply troubled by these messages and their probable consequences. 'Now, what do you expect of somebody you treat as though they were nothing? They either fight back or they crawl into a shell and become nothing.'

Experiences such as these had left Darrelle with a deep awareness of the fragility of each child's sensibilities, the awesome power that teachers potentially wield and the impact that this can have, for better or worse, on children's sense of themselves as learners, on their sense of their place in the school's scheme of things. Consequently she avowed an almost parental belief in every child's worth, as well as a responsibility to communicate this belief to every child in her class. 'Jo and I spend all our time,' Darrelle said, 'trying to build our children up, make them think they're wonderful and loved and they're clever and can do anything.' The possible tension between the aim of releasing children from dependence on the teacher's approval on the one hand, and constantly feeding them positive messages on the other, can be resolved if we understand that Darrelle's priority was to communicate worth through personal recognition rather than through praise. What was important was that all children should feel known and appreciated as themselves, not for compliant behaviour or specific accomplishments.

This sense of personal recognition was communicated partly through the attentiveness with which Darrelle listened to her children, engaged with their ideas and took what they had to say seriously. It was also communicated through empathy, through her willingness to step outside her own perspective and try to see the world of school from the children's point of view. Schon (1988) talks about the importance of 'giving children reason', by which he means starting out from the assumption that what the child is doing or saying makes sense, even if at first the teacher does not understand the child's meaning. The teacher's own understanding grows as she tries to step outside her own frames of reference and penetrate that meaning from the child's perspective. Darrelle's commitment to empathetic relationships helped her to release children from constraints that might otherwise limit their learning. For example, two children in her class asked to choose their own books to read, instead of being directed to particular books, colour-coded for levels of difficulty. Darrelle was initially reluctant to agree. On further reflection, however, she sensed that one child's request might stem from his feeling that he was 'rubbish' at reading; from his perspective, she might seem to be confirming this judgement – and so the emotional block that it was creating – if she insisted that he continue to make his choices from a particular level. So she invited him to select his own reading matter, while watching carefully over his choice of books and his progress. She was gratified to see that within a short time he began to read much more fluently and confidently. Another child appeared to be deeply motivated by her parents' challenge to become a 'free reader' – a classroom shorthand term for someone who chooses books freely, having read all the colour-coded material. Darrelle felt that it was right to capitalize on this ambition rather than discouraging it. Her capacity to step into this girl's shoes and appreciate what would make a difference from her point of view was rewarded: she observed that this child progressed 'in leaps and bounds' once she was given the freedom to choose her own books.

However, staff were well aware that this process of coming to know and give recognition to each child individually requires ongoing work. It can never be taken for granted or left to chance. The more freedom that was extended to learners and the more control they were able to exercise over their learning, the more unpredictable learning became. It was all the more vital, then, to be continually seeking to understand the meaning of the child's activities from the child's point of view. Empathy, including listening to children, was a vital tool for teachers who, as Simon said, must always see themselves and present themselves to children as continually learning. Children in Jo's Year 5 class were clearly beginning to take seriously their responsibility for helping her to gain insight into their thinking and behaviour. In her thesis, Jo describes a moment of true partnership when Louis confided, 'I think a lot. It looks like I'm daydreaming but I'm not. I'm thinking, but it takes a long time!' (Smith 2007: 47).

Insights arising from the recent classroom observational study, referred to in Chapter 3, stress the necessarily incomplete knowledge of children with which teachers must always work. Bibby (2011) uses a psychoanalytical lens to make sense of her observations of teacher–pupil interactions in a class of learners in their last two years of primary school. Communication between teachers and children is never going to be completely transparent, she argues. 'But if we work together, we may come to know each other a little better . . . To know the other, to hold them in mind, requires that we step beyond ourselves' (Bibby 2011: 132).

In the same study, Bibby also discusses the importance of creating 'holding environments' for learners, allowing them to confront difficulties and challenges, knowing that tensions and anxieties will pass, rather than coming to the rescue with less challenging work or premature assistance that reduces opportunities for learning. Wroxham teachers talked about how they could anticipate feelings and reactions that might be a barrier to children's whole-hearted engagement, and worked out ways to acknowledge and address these in their build-up to an activity. For example, when Simon and Martyn jointly taught the series of writing lessons described in Chapter 3, they anticipated that some children might experience some fears about working together. Rightly so, as Alison discovered when she sat with the Year 4 children just before the lesson began. The children expressed their deep apprehensions about working with the older children, especially about exposing what they felt to be their limited writing skills.

When the two classes came together, Martyn and Simon began by illustrating their own learning through sharing amusing stories about their ongoing attempts to learn to play golf. The message to the children was that learning can be difficult, however experienced you are. They planned this introduction deliberately, because they wanted the children in the two different year groups to approach the task of working together in an open-minded way. Since everybody was still learning, there was scope for older and younger children to learn productively together. The older children did not need to feel that they knew best and the younger children needed to understand that their ideas would be heard and built upon. In this way everybody was being helped to see how writing together would enable the production of a piece of work that individuals could not have achieved alone. Through their stories, Simon and Martyn prepared the children to try out a different way of working, partnering people from a different age group, encouraging them to understand that it was worth taking the risk because 'We're learning to be good citizens.' Everyone could support and help everyone else; making mistakes and overcoming them was all part of learning. 'We're not just teaching them to write,' Simon explained, 'we're teaching them to be people.'

Across the school, there was a general recognition that learning does not take place when there are emotional problems such as worries about home, or conflict between friends. Several classes provided home-made post boxes, through which children could tell about their personal feelings. In our discussion of the learning journals kept by Year 5 children in Chapter 3, we noted that these could be used to confide about friendships or any other worries, as well as issues related to learning. The comment below was written in a journal at a time when some of the girls were finding it difficult to sustain friendships:

> I don't like telling my mum what's happened at school unless it's major! Because if I tell my mum it means there is somewhere else where I get upset. Everyone is having lots of little silly arguments and it's breaking up friendships. It's been going on for ages and I feel like we can't have a day without arguing.

Several teachers expressed the belief that emotions and feelings should be openly acknowledged, as a way of helping children to move on from any difficulties. The children echoed this view. A Year 6 child, just about to leave the school, looked back and noted with appreciation that her class teacher 'knows when you are upset and she knows how to make you feel better so you can learn . . . she notices things very quickly so if you come in one day and maybe you're feeling different she can spot that out really quickly'.

Awareness that the school environment needed to offer support for emotional issues led to discussion in circle group meetings about how such support could be provided. It was agreed to turn the medical room into a quiet place where people could go if they needed a 'calming down space' or simply felt sad. The room was redecorated and furnished with soft chairs, teddies, books and cushions. A local resident made a large rainbow collage that was suspended from the ceiling. In circle group meetings, the children voted to rename it the Rainbow Room. In theory children could go to the Rainbow Room unsupervised for some time on their own. In fact, the location of the room just opposite the school office ensured that any child choosing to take 'time out' was noted by the office team and unobtrusively monitored in case an adult might be needed to offer support. Use of the room varied according to stresses experienced by individual children, but the provision of this space continues to be highly valued by everybody.

Empathy on the part of the teaching team was a route to creative thinking and problem solving across all aspects of children's experiences in school. Difficulties arising with social relationships and children's sense of belonging were taken just as seriously as issues around academic progress or classroom behaviour, since staff understood that difficulties in these areas could have such a powerful effect on children's overall well-being and learning. For example, Lizzy was a quiet, shy member of the Year 6 class. During the latter stages of Year 5 it had become apparent that she was finding it difficult to socialize with her peers because she had few interests in common with them. As a result, she was becoming reluctant to come to school. In response, the adults at her learning review meeting suggested something that they hoped might stimulate a new interest and sense of purpose. The head and deputy invited her to take on a school-wide responsibility for some BBC Children in Need fundraising events. They explained that she would need to plan these events through the circle group meetings and then organize them, possibly with the help of a small working group. Lizzy seemed to like the idea and her mother offered encouragement.

As a result of this imaginative response to her problem, Lizzy established a new friendship with Karen, another quiet member of the class. They met after school at each other's houses to discuss their ideas and took their plans to the circle group meetings. Together, they made posters, presented the ideas generated in the circle groups to a whole-school assembly and organized a successful bring and buy sale. These fundraising events generated a great enthusiasm throughout the school, and the girls were interviewed for the local newspaper. The success of the initiative was indicative of how well the adults involved had been able to put themselves into Lizzy's shoes and invent a way of involving her in a high-profile event that so skilfully harnessed her strengths and interests.

Empathy also guided staff's responses to the challenges presented by David who joined the school when he was 9. Although he initially seemed to make friends on the playground, he found it difficult to keep his temper, particularly during competitive games such as football. An audience of curious children would rapidly gather if David showed signs of becoming angry and their attention could quickly escalate the situation. The Year 6 children who organized games for the younger ones found David very hard to deal with; on one occasion he lost his temper and hit one of the playground staff hard with a cricket bat. This incident led to David being excluded for half a day, which everybody knew was an unsustainable and undesirable form of response.

When Jo, his class teacher, talked to David, it became clear that he disliked the feelings of anger that welled up within him but found it almost impossible to control himself once these feelings had been triggered. Through talking with him and trying to understand his anxieties, it was discovered that David was an expert in caring for guinea pigs. At this time, it was unusual for schools to allow animals to be cared for on the premises due to strict health and safety regulations. However, it was decided that a hutch for two guinea pigs should be installed near his classroom so that David could care for the animals during the lunch hour, and help other children learn how to look after them. When the new guinea pigs, Ant and Dec, arrived in school there was great excitement. They lived in the courtyard overlooked by the school café and children of all ages delighted in watching them through the window while eating lunch. The children's interest in David's tantrums declined, as they preferred the privilege of spending time with him while he cared for the school pets.

The approach taken to help David seems to illustrate what Salmon (1995: 80) means when she advocates 'making more generous room within our schooling system' in order to accommodate *all* young people, including those perceived as 'different'. Schools need to set aside the 'language of complaint', she suggests, in response to challenging behaviour, and focus instead on the 'perspectives, the personal subjectivities, of children themselves'. Although this child had hurt others and even struck a member of staff, he was not demonized. The chosen solution was uniquely tailored to David's strengths as a person. It created a positive space in which he could affirm and build his sense of self as a competent, caring human being, and be accepted and recognized as such by staff and children. Although he had shown anger and violence he was trusted to care for vulnerable creatures. Younger children would come to ask him if they could visit the animals, enabling him to act as a caring, informative guide. In finding a way for him to make a positive contribution to the school, the staff clearly signalled that David and, by implication, everybody is worthy of another chance and that everybody can be a valued member of the community when given the right opportunities.

As well as benefiting David, the solution created a ripple effect that spread out across the whole community. It modelled for children some important messages about relationships, about how people do and should treat one another at Wroxham. It helped to build empathy within the community generally. Although David continued to present the school team with many challenges, people found themselves more able to empathize with David, to hope and trust that he would gradually bring his temper under control.

Maintaining steadfastness of purpose

Work to develop relationships in the ways described so far in this chapter was always complex and demanding. However, as long as things were progressing relatively smoothly, it was also deeply rewarding to see how children responded to the efforts of the teaching team. It was not difficult to hold on to convictions about the kinds of relationships needed to enable freedom to learn and continue to foster them. It was when crises arose that values and principles were tested to the limits. We saw how close Sophie came to breaking point, and how important it was to the eventual outcome that she did not waver in her resolve. Within the school community generally, it was often behaviour that created the greatest challenge. The need to respond instantly to ensure everyone's safety could pre-empt responses congruent with the kinds of relationships to which the teaching team increasingly aspired.

A particular challenge to staff arose when it was decided to allow Miles, a looked-after child, to enter the nursery two terms early, once staff knew about his circumstances and saw how he reacted on his first visit to the nursery. Miles, who had just begun a new foster placement, had spent his first years in a highly restricted environment with limited interaction and very few play opportunities. His first visit to the nursery was memorable. When he was taken to the outdoor area he tore his hand away from his foster mother and ran towards the children playing. He was so excited by a play car that he could not resist climbing aboard. The child who was driving gave up the car when Miles leant through the window and stroked his hair gently while muttering urgently and gazing longingly at the steering wheel. However, no sooner had he gained possession of the vehicle than he spied a playhouse. Leaving the car, he approached the house and dived head first through the window, not waiting to open the door. His frantic delight in the company of children and the wealth of play resources demonstrated how much he would benefit from joining the setting immediately.

Miles had very limited understanding of physical danger and was consequently assigned a one-to-one key worker straight away. Working with Miles was challenging. Physically, he had difficulty with coordination and would often stumble or fall. Socially, he often found it difficult to participate with the other children. Sometimes he expressed distress or frustration physically, for instance by biting or scratching. In the early days, there were times when the Foundation Stage team wondered if, with Miles, they had reached the limits of their acceptance. Was this the right place for Miles after all? However, they worked together and closely supported Sam, his key worker. The headteacher helped by providing a 'holding environment' for the Foundation team, talking issues through with them and making available practical support, for example time out to meet and talk with Miles' carer. This shared commitment enabled the team to stay strong even when it felt as though Miles' progress was impossibly slow.

Gradually, as they began to know Miles, their trust that they could enable him to belong and learn in that environment began to grow. He began to communicate, using a few words, and to show understanding of the rules of the setting. He began to take on the role of class 'policeman' echoing comments from the adults. During one observation the nursery teacher told a group of children not to add any more water to the 'gloop'; this was immediately echoed by Miles' shout from across the room 'No more water with it!' On most days the support Miles received from his key worker enabled him to join in with the vast majority of nursery activities.

For the children, the process of 'making generous room' for Miles as a full member of their community happened quite readily. In an interview, Sam spoke very positively about how he was treated by other children. 'They simplify their own words so he understands,' she observed. 'They're extremely accepting of him.' She went on to explain that in the busy nursery setting 'he learns the most from observing the other children . . . he's learning the same things the other children are learning, he just needs more support doing it'.

Challenges to the relationships that the teaching team aspired to develop also occasionally arose in contacts with parents. Although working in close partnership with families was an aim of the school, there were times when this required courage and resilience. On one occasion, the police were called when a parent sought help from the headteacher following allegations of road-rage attacks against her by another parent. On another occasion, a parent insisted on an immediate meeting with Alison, threatening violence if this was not arranged. Alison acknowledged that aggressive behaviour and threats were very hard to cope with. Conflict is often deep-rooted, sometimes the result of a parent's own experience of school or a belief that a child is being unfairly treated, unnoticed or misunderstood. There were times when although the easier option would have been to refuse to engage, it was more important to try to build shared understanding and to listen. There is a toy wooden crocodile on the coffee table in the headteacher's room, with a big grin and a closed mouth. Alison bought it after only a few weeks of headship, to remind her that it is often more powerful to listen than to talk. It is difficult to spend time listening to complaints and criticisms while trying to move a school forward, but a listening school has to do just that. Alison believed that hearing people's concerns and acting upon them were the only way that trust between the school and its community could be established.

Maintaining steadfastness of purpose in the most challenging situations required collective effort. As we saw in the account of the Foundation team's work with Miles, it was partly because people pulled together and supported one another that the team together found the strength to hold on to their principles and take the steps needed to 'make generous room' for Miles within their learning community. Looking for solutions congruent with their principles also required creativity, because each new situation needed its own unique solution. However, as time went on, and experience grew, the search for solutions became supported by what Alison referred to as the staff's 'collective memory'. Although no two situations were ever the same, staff were able to look back and draw both confidence and inspiration from how similar situations had been successfully tackled previously. What they learned from previously creative solutions became the springboard for finding principled and constructive ways forward.

Making connections

In this chapter we have explored what staff at Wroxham were doing to build the kinds of relationships that they felt were needed in order to foster their key aim of extending freedom to learn. As we have identified and discussed four common elements of this work, shared understandings, acceptance, empathy and steadfastness of purpose, we have drawn on the ideas of Rogers to help us to understand and appreciate the significance of the developments that were taking place. Rogers argued that for autonomous learning to be possible, the relationship between teachers and children needs to be non-threatening and accepting. Such a relationship has four key characteristics:

- The teacher values the child, showing care and respect for the individuality of each child.
- The teacher trusts the child, believing that the child has the desire and the potentiality to learn and grow.
- The teacher empathizes with the child, seeking to view the world and the process of learning through the child's eyes.
- The teacher is himself, trying to be genuine and honest, not performing a role, a real person rather than a front or a façade.

(Adapted from Hargreaves 1972: 216–17)

None of the staff, including the headteacher, referred to Rogers' work as a source for their thinking about relationships, nor did they explicitly use the language of 'acceptance'. Yet their values, understandings and the course of their learning had, it seems, brought them, individually and collectively, to views very similar to Rogers' own. In our analysis, we have not specifically addressed the characteristic of genuineness, but on reflection we can see that many of our chosen examples do also reveal teachers deliberately choosing to present themselves as real people – people who are continually learning, who make mistakes, who do not know everything, who are human, who have lives, families and interests outside school.

As well as helping us to make the connection between the different kinds of work on relationships and the core purpose of extending freedom to learn, Rogers' insights also help us to see how those developments connect with the *Learning without Limits* ethos that the headteacher was seeking to foster. Rogers' ideas, and the research that supports them, draw attention to dramatic changes that can be brought about in the quality of learners' engagement in classroom activity through changes in relationships. Research undertaken for Rogers' 1983 edition of *Freedom to Learn* (General Teaching Council website 2008) found that when teachers provided the kind of emotionally supportive, facilitative climate Rogers describes, students learned more, enjoyed lessons and attended school more regularly. They were also more creative, asked more questions, were more involved in learning, more capable of problem solving, and demonstrated more spontaneity, initiative and independence. As we have shown, these were exactly the kinds of attitudes and dispositions that the Wroxham teachers were seeking to foster.

We can see, therefore, how work on relationships at Wroxham connects with the *Learning without Limits* core idea of 'transformability'. Embedded in that work is the conviction that people – adults and children – can bring about even dramatic changes in future patterns of learning and behaviour through their choices and actions in the present. Everything that happens in the present has an impact, for better or worse, on how things develop in future. Wroxham teachers' understanding of what they could do, in the domain of relationships, to create even better conditions for learning, free from the constraints of ability labelling, is reflected in the four areas of work identified.

First, we can appreciate more clearly why classroom dialogue was frequently concerned with ideas about learning and what good learners do. If ideas of fixed ability permeate classroom thinking and practices, the topic of how to be a good learner, or become a better learner, is unlikely to figure in ongoing discussion. Since by definition only some learners are 'good', and whether particular children are good learners or not is not something they can do much about, teachers are unlikely to engage their classes at any length in discussion about how to be a good learner. As teachers progressively abandoned ability-based thinking, the topic of how to be a good learner necessarily became an urgent priority for *everybody*. Teachers recognized the need to spend time talking with children and helping them to develop confidence and belief in their capacity to learn, and in the things that they could do, alone and in collaboration, to enhance their power as learners.

Secondly, we can see how the shared understandings and experiences that led to the progressive abandonment of ability-based thinking and practices *also* led naturally to the construction of non-threatening, accepting relationships based on trust. Ability labels, by their very nature, deprive teachers and children of trust in most children's learning capacity. They institute a hierarchy of expectations, and a regime of constant comparison and monitoring, to ensure that the attainments of children of different presumed abilities progress in line with their perceived potential. While teachers may believe that good, trusting relationships are important and work hard to create them, fear is an endemic feature of classrooms where ability-focused ideas and practices persist. Indeed, a long series of ingenious studies by Dweck and her colleagues has shown that even those who earn the coveted 'high ability' label can be inhibited rather than encouraged in their learning because of the fear of losing it (Dweck 2008: 45). Underlying developments at Wroxham was an awareness that reconstructing classroom relationships based on trust, trusting *all* children to be 'essentially competent human beings' (Rogers and Freiberg 1994: 43), was potentially transformative, freeing teachers and children from the limitations created by ability judgements. However, as the teaching teams also clearly appreciated, realizing that potential requires ongoing work. Trust strengthens through experience. As teachers and children give and receive trust in their day-to-day interactions, not only do they find their sense of trust becoming more firmly rooted; they also expand their understandings of what is possible, what *becomes* possible, in a climate in which everybody's learning is sustained by accepting and trusting relationships.

Thirdly, we can also appreciate the connection between the progressive abandonment of ability thinking and the focus, at Wroxham, on establishing empathy at the heart of teaching and learning relationships. Ability labels provide a means of 'knowing' children by classifying them. Individuals' attainments are graded and calibrated against nationally imposed benchmarks; the place they occupy on the attainment ladder then becomes equated with their presumed ability. These classifications inform future expectations and planning for each child. All the other rich information that teachers gather about children in their classes tends to be sidelined. As teachers move away from the use of ability categories and grouping by attainment or ability, and as trust in children as active thinkers and meaning-makers in their own right grows, teachers naturally give more importance to other ways of knowing children. These other ways include, perhaps most importantly, trying to understand the child's reasoning, difficulties, purposes, hopes and fears from the child's point of view. This process, as we have seen, inevitably requires ongoing work. It requires considerable effort on the part of the teacher to try to penetrate the complex, diverse worlds of children's experience, as Salmon acknowledges in her fascinating study of the application of personal construct psychology to classroom learning. Teachers have to work to extend the limits of 'sociality', their 'broad and sensitive attention to how another construes his world' if they are 'to extend more widely the invitation that teaching essentially entails' (Salmon 1995: 38).

Finally, work to maintain steadfastness of purpose links to the *Learning without Limits* core ideas because it helps to ensure that the principles guiding developments are applied to *everybody*, without exception. Whereas ability categories reify differences and make it seem legitimate for different principles to be applied to supposedly different kinds of children, at Wroxham, increasingly, no such distinctions were accepted. No one was written off. Even in the most challenging situations, people looked for creative ways of making generous room for everybody to be accepted, for everybody to feel that they belonged and for everybody to flourish.

5 Putting learning first: creating a school-wide culture of learning

In Chapter 2 we explored some of the structures introduced in the early days of Alison's headship that laid foundations for an alternative approach to school development. We found embedded in those structures the core *Learning without Limits* principles that guided Alison's leadership and noted that her approach was based on trust that, given the right conditions and support, colleagues would be stimulated to do their own thinking, without being directed towards particular strategies and practices. In Chapters 3 and 4 we looked in detail at some of the developments in teachers' thinking and practices that evolved during the period of the research, and saw how work in the area of relationships was crucially important in these developments. Many of the changes taking place clearly had their roots in the contexts created by the new structures. However, it would be wrong to imply that these structures, in themselves, were sufficient to nurture and sustain continuing development work. Trust in the teaching team did not mean that the headteacher simply stood back and waited for learning to happen. On the contrary, she explained that there was important ongoing work to be done: namely, to create the conditions for the growth of a school-wide culture of learning which would support everybody's learning and foster developments in thinking and practice within the teaching team, individually and collectively. In this chapter we explore the nature of the leadership task in creating this school-wide culture of learning. We examine the range of strategies employed and how a stable environment was created to free everybody to focus on learning. We draw out how these strategies were helping to build a strong community of professional learners, while also engaging children and parents as active participants in the life of the school. We conclude by recognizing the important moral underpinnings that increasingly have come to inspire the work of whole-school development.

In exploring the role of leadership in this chapter, we are drawing primarily on the headteacher's thinking and experiences as recorded in her journal and interviews, and comments that staff made about her leadership. This is not to imply that Alison was the only person exercising leadership during this period. Alison would be the first to say that the tasks of leadership were carried out through teamwork; however, it is still important to explore the role of the headteacher in shaping the nature of school development and professional learning. We focus first and principally on what was done, in building the school-wide culture, to foster the learning of the staff team. Later in the chapter, we consider how these developments also helped to engage children, parents, governors and all members of the school community.

The leadership role in building a school-wide culture of learning

With respect to the teaching team, the leadership task Alison set herself was, in essence, to foster the learning of staff, individually and collectively, through a focus on children's learning; it was to encourage colleagues to take pride in their own and each other's capacity to learn, and to treat this as integral to their professional identity. The approach that Alison adopted was subtle and non-didactic. It ranged from working closely with colleagues to support them, to facilitating learning through contact with the ideas of others. When she was involved directly in supporting staff learning, she positioned herself alongside colleagues, offering her experience as a partner in learning rather than as an expert with all the answers. She ensured that the focus of her conversations and collaborative work with staff was always firmly on children's learning, assuming that a passionate interest in children's learning was something that they could all share; questions relating to curriculum, pedagogy and assessment were always explored in a context that was of immediate relevance and importance to individual colleagues and to their work with children.

In order to engage fruitfully in these conversations, Alison needed to stay close to what was happening in the classroom. To this end she frequently spent time in every classroom, not in a monitoring role (giving feedback about teachers' performance or identifying areas for improvement), but focusing on children's learning. This focus helped her to build the knowledge, understandings and relationships that would be the basis of her contribution to staff learning. These classroom observations prompted and sustained ongoing dialogue between Alison and the teaching team rooted in shared experiences; they helped her to make delicate judgements about when more active support and input might be helpful in fostering learning. Furthermore, in her contributions to these conversations, Alison helped to develop ways of talking about children's learning without reference to notions of ability or levels of attainment; she tried to ensure that these shared reflections focused on children's present powers as learners, and on how these could be further strengthened and extended. As these discussions about children's learning became increasingly woven into the fabric of the school community, staff naturally took the initiative to come to Alison to talk about questions and issues arising in their work with children. Whatever the origin of the conversation, Alison's response was always to value what people were already doing and to listen to them, rather than telling them what to do. In this way, she could understand them and their work, tuning in to what was important to them. She could find ways of coming alongside them to share their thinking; from this position, she was well placed to suggest possible developments in practice that colleagues talked over with her.

However, significant leadership activities that contributed to the development of a school-wide culture of learning did not necessarily entail direct involvement. Indeed, leadership interventions were often made at one or more removes from the thinking and learning of the staff team. The work of leading the school entailed *creating conditions* that supported and stimulated professional learning. As Alison said, 'I create the conditions and they do the learning.'

We are not suggesting that at the beginning of her headship Alison formally articulated these leadership strategies as a blueprint for change. As we noted in Chapter 1, Alison saw herself as working largely intuitively at this time. Her repertoire of strategies developed over a number of years, and the thematic structure presented in Figure 5.1 emerged through the research process. The four main groups of strategies are explored in detail below.

Collaborating and supporting

One example of how Alison's contribution followed through from an initial conversation to active involvement was Martyn's Robin Hood Day, described in Chapter 3. This collaboration began when Martyn talked to Alison about his concerns that some of the 8- and 9-year-olds in his class did not seem to have many ideas for writing and were reluctant to write. Alison recalled listening to his concern, and giving him a book about children's writing that she hoped would give him some rich food for thought (Armstrong 2006); they talked through some of the things that affect children's desire to write. Alison did not give advice or make specific suggestions about what Martyn might do. She left him with the question 'What could you do to make writing irresistible for them?' A day or two later, he put his head round Alison's door and told her his plan for a Robin Hood Day. Alison responded enthusiastically to his ideas, supporting and encouraging his emerging interest in learning outdoors. On the day itself, she made a number of visits to the field and nearby woodland to talk to the children and to ensure that all was going well, since she was aware that the open-ended outdoor situation presented some risks both for Martyn and for the children. The following day, she wrote a letter to the children to say how impressed she was that they had worked so well as a team, and that she was looking forward to seeing their writing.

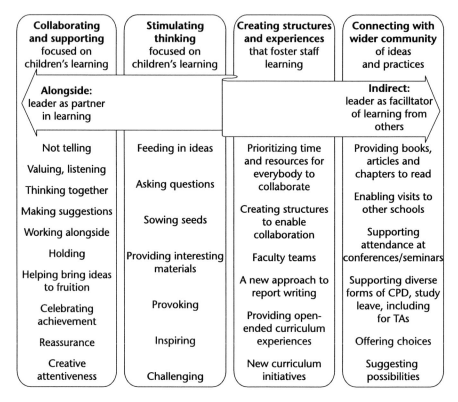

Figure 5.1 The range of strategies used in building a school-wide culture of learning

She also made it clear to Martyn that she genuinely shared his own delight in the success of the day and in the children's enthusiasm, putting a letter in his post tray to thank him for giving the children such a wonderful experience.

Encouraging writing, this time in the reception class, provided another context for Alison's active involvement. Sarah, a member of the Year R teaching team, was doing a special study of children's writing as part of her Foundation degree course in education. She had been talking to Alison about this study and about 4-year-old Fay, who could and did write with her mother at home, but did not choose to write in school. For much of her time in the Foundation Stage, Fay had chosen to spend her time in other areas of provision, such as outdoor and messy activities and role-play with friends. She was more interested in socializing than in demonstrating her knowledge of writing. Sarah and the Foundation team were wondering if they ought to be doing more to encourage Fay to write in school. They talked with Alison about their concerns and concluded that Fay's chosen activities were important parts of the early years curriculum. There was no reason to pressurize Fay to write in school, just because they knew that she could. They trusted that Fay would start writing of her own accord. Meanwhile, in discussion with Alison about giving children reasons to want to write, they decided to create conditions that might make the activity of writing more appealing. They decided that it would be exciting for the children to receive a letter from the headteacher, and hoped they would be moved to reply. Sarah accordingly set up a post box in the role-play area, and Fay joined other children in sending letters in answer to the headteacher. Although she could write, Fay, like the other children, chose to do signed drawings. Alison pinned up the drawings in her office and replied, in her turn, by sending a letter to the class via the post box that included a photograph of the display.

Over the next few weeks, more letters passed to and fro; Fay, with other children, continued to send their signed pictures to Alison. Only when Alison wrote to Fay personally, including a photograph of her cat, and asking if she had any pets, was Fay moved to write a response.

> Dear Mrs Peacock
> We hav got 2 cats called Dinah And Pip
> Love from Fay

These two examples illustrate the emerging synergy between adult learning and children's learning. Creative collaboration with members of the teaching team led to carefully planned strategies to extend and enhance learning opportunities. The children's engagement with these new experiences in turn yielded new insights into what affects motivation, what enables writing, the importance of respecting children's choices and how to balance curricular priorities. These themes continued to be thought about and worked at in an ongoing way, rather than being solved or sorted definitively. Part of the leadership task was to keep a mental log of the topics and issues being explored by staff, not only to keep the conversations going, but also so that Alison could bring together colleagues whose thinking was focused on similar areas to share ideas and practices.

Another active leadership contribution was to ensure that resources were made available to support exciting and innovative ideas. So, for instance, when staff expressed their concern that some children seemed to have no idea where vegetables came from, a lunchtime play-leader and a governor volunteered to establish a lunchtime gardening club, so that children could grow their own vegetables and then sell their fresh produce. When a teacher decided to turn her role-play area into an optician's consulting room, Alison visited local opticians and collected a fascinating array of spectacle frames and charts. When Jo decided, with her class, to hold a Celtic day and build a Celtic hut on the school field instead of visiting a museum, the site manager's knowledge, expertise and enthusiasm were enlisted to assist with its construction. Tapping into the human resources of the collective in this way helped to ensure that the team offered children more engaging and authentic learning experiences, while also guiding colleagues' thinking along these particular lines. When people saw for themselves how positively the children responded to these experiences, they were able to draw out implications about the kinds of learning experiences that they might provide in future. Alison's contributions did not merely support one-off events; there was also the potential for staff to grasp generalizable insights that would inform their future thinking and teaching.

There were occasionally circumstances when the decision to become actively involved with one or more members of staff was less a matter of delicate judgement than of necessity. In Chapter 4, we saw how Bibby (2011), who observed teacher-pupil interactions in a class of learners in their last two years of primary school, emphasizes the importance of creating a 'holding environment' for learners. A parallel can be drawn between 'holding' in the context of children's learning and Alison's approach to supporting the learning of the teaching team, particularly in challenging situations. We showed, for example, in Chapter 4, how she was able to help the Foundation Stage team with Miles, a child whose behaviour they found very challenging, and how the team was helped to stay strong by knowing that they were being 'held in mind'. Recalling her own role in working with the team, Alison said that she mostly spent time with them reflecting on what was happening, helping them to read the clues in Miles's behaviour, helping to develop a shared understanding of how best to enable his participation and learning. She made sure she was well informed about their concerns by regularly spending time in the nursery, sometimes visiting twice in a session, and listening to their comments on the events of the day. When the team was in danger of being overwhelmed by the challenges they met, she increased her input, not to take over but to intensify her support.

Providing a 'holding environment' for staff in challenging situations enabled people to persist with their efforts, trusting in Alison's capacity to keep them safe. She did not offer to rescue them, or to do their work for them, but held things stable until they found their own solutions. As we saw, pulling together gave the team the strength to hold on to their principles and take the steps needed to 'make generous room' for Miles within their learning community. Alison, though hesitant to use the metaphor, likened this part of her role to the way a parent supports a child, so that the child feels 'you can get on with what you need to do . . . because someone is there looking after you and making sure that it's all going to be ok. And that sounds silly, but . . . it is important, because the job of teaching children is such a demanding job.'

Stimulating thinking

At one remove from direct, collaborative involvement with colleagues and children, there were leadership activities where the intention, in conversations about learning, was to stimulate colleagues to think along particular lines, without necessarily expecting anything immediate to result. Alison said 'It's about feeding things in that people can take on and develop in their own way.' Sophie noted her own appreciation of this strategy when she commented, 'Alison is very clever at making you reflect . . . she doesn't actually tell you anything, but she asks you questions.' Reflecting takes place over time and in a variety of contexts; then, once people have had a chance to think things through for themselves, they can use their new ideas in ways that make sense to them.

If we look more closely at recorded occasions when the leadership strategy took the form of stimulating thinking, we can begin to identify some of the important directions in which people's thinking was being encouraged. For instance, when Alison mentioned the apple tree to Sarah (see Chapter 2), she was not merely drawing attention to a specific first-hand experience that was too good to miss but, in more general terms, encouraging thinking about learning about the real world, and the many exciting learning opportunities waiting to be discovered in the immediate outdoor environment. The sceptical reader may see Alison's suggestion 'Wouldn't it be lovely if . . .' as communicating an invitation it would be better not to refuse rather than as offering a genuine choice; however, it really would not have mattered to Alison if Sarah had not taken up the idea on this particular occasion. It was worthwhile in itself that the conversation about the tree took place, inviting her colleague to empathize with the excitement that finding it might create for the children. Alison was gently guiding thinking in particular directions: sowing seeds that she trusted would take root, if not now, then in the future.

Similarly, when Alison raised the question 'How can we enable them to experience dark?' in the context of the 'Light and Dark' project discussed in Chapter 3, she was, once again, encouraging colleagues to think about the importance of giving children the opportunity to learn through authentic experience. Recognizing the need, following it through in the context of this particular project and seeing how the children responded, gave staff the opportunity to deepen their appreciation of the importance of children learning from first-hand experience *through their own* first-hand experiences. Alison worked to avoid situations where colleagues could feel compromised by having to take an idea up, or by feeling that there was a right or wrong way of proceeding. In her own words, 'It's about recognizing that you've sown a seed somewhere.' She stimulated colleagues' thinking in ways that allowed them freedom and control over deciding whether or how to take ideas on.

In addition to asking questions and making suggestions, a further leadership strategy was to provide interesting materials and invite teaching staff to come up with inventive ways of using them to inspire learning. In Chapter 2, we described an exciting investigation that Jo developed with her Year 2 class using a collection of Victorian glass bottles that Alison bought at a car boot sale. We noted how other members of the teaching team were invited into the classroom to share in the children's excitement and to celebrate their achievements. Another example of an intriguing resource was a wooden boat installed in the playground area adjacent to the Year 3 classroom. The teaching team were planning a term's work on global exploration and Alison was keen that the outdoor environment should be recognized as an extension of the classroom. The idea of buying a real boat that could be set into the ground became a reality when one came up for sale on an internet auction site. A wooden canoe with trailer was purchased, collected by the site manager and fixed to the ground during the summer holidays. When children returned to school in September, one of the first things they saw as they arrived in the playground was the boat. The intention was not that this resource should be used for specific teaching purposes, but that its presence would serve as an invitation to the imagination of both children and adults.

Delicate judgement was always needed to ensure that questions, suggestions and provocations were carefully chosen and timed if teaching staff were to find themselves able to take up their freedom to think for themselves. Alison recognized the necessity of going with the grain of people's thinking if her questions and challenges were to foster creativity in building a rich, enticing curriculum, while ensuring that colleagues retained ownership of their own professional learning and practice. Operating largely intuitively, she was discovering how to lead her staff in ways that were congruent with her principles. She was very aware, as we shall see, that she needed to evolve strategies to support her own learning as well as that of colleagues. By nourishing her own learning, a process which she shared with her colleagues, she avoided positioning herself as the expert, while at the same time enriching conditions for everybody's learning.

Creating structures and experiences that foster staff learning

A further strategy was to prioritize time and resources to allow people to work together, share ideas and learn from each other. Alison was determined that staff should never feel isolated or alone with their own class of children. Instead, people were encouraged to meet together to discuss ideas, to think about the learning of particular children and to take collective responsibility for everybody's learning. They were encouraged to ask questions about their practice, and to share the conundrums they were tussling with. In discussions and encounters like these, they were able to help each other to reflect. The very process of attempting to articulate what they were struggling with, Alison said, increased their understanding.

In Chapter 2 we described how Alison began to create collaborative structures (circle group meetings, faculty teams and learning review meetings) that provided rich, open-ended contexts in which colleagues could learn with and from each other, and with and from parents and children. In addition to these early initiatives, which continued to flourish and evolve during the period of the research, a major leadership task was to organize and resource weekly planning meetings for all teaching staff working with a particular class. Although release time for planning and preparation has become a statutory entitlement for teachers in all maintained schools (Department for Education and Skills 2002), it is rare for release to be organized specifically to enable collaborative thinking and learning, and exceptionally rare for teaching assistants to be released, during the school day, to meet and plan regularly with teachers. At Wroxham, it was a high priority to enable *everybody* working with a class of children to share regularly in evaluation and planning. Teaching assistants were not present simply to be informed about curriculum plans for the following week. The aim was to facilitate a genuine exchange of ideas, attributing value to and drawing on each person's knowledge of the children to contribute to shared thinking about how to take learning forward.

Teaching teams were released together for half a day, whenever possible, to review and evaluate the previous week's learning and plan for the following week. If student teachers were working with the class, they automatically joined the meeting. One teacher also included children in the planning team, with small groups of children, in rotation, offering their thoughts about the week's experiences and suggestions for the week ahead. Alison admitted that it was a logistical challenge to organize simultaneous release for all members of a team, to manage the resource implications, and ensure that the quality of children's learning experiences was sustained while the teaching teams were meeting. In the Foundation Stage, it was not possible for everybody to meet at the same time because of the children's need for the continuous presence of familiar people. Nevertheless, across the school generally, support from the teaching teams for joint planning was so great that everybody contributed to organizing it, sitting down together with large sheets of paper to construct a workable timetable and solving problems as they arose. The same substitute teacher, a maths and art specialist, covered all the release time for planning, preparation and assessment.

Opportunities for collaborative learning were also organized within the faculty teams. When a faculty team was planning a specific initiative related to its area of responsibility, details were shared with staff in other teams, inviting them to come and observe the activities in particular year groups. Release was organized to enable these visits to take place, and the observations were followed up by conversations between the observers and the host teaching team. Because staff knew that there was strong leadership support for collaboration, they also often initiated their own opportunities to learn together by working alongside one another. In Chapter 3, we noted how Simon and Martyn brought their classes together to write play scripts. This activity necessarily required joint thinking before the event; it created many opportunities for them to observe and learn from each other while they were team-teaching; it also created a powerful shared experience, which provided the basis for further conversations about enabling writing.

A new approach to report writing, another rich collaborative context for staff learning from and with children, evolved from the learning review meetings described in Chapter 2. It was initiated by Simon who, with the time of year for report writing approaching, found himself feeling uncomfortable with the format currently in use at Wroxham. He concluded that writing a summative report at the end of the year, summarizing how well each child had done, did not reflect the partnership approach to learning based on listening to children that staff had been developing, as summarized in Chapter 3. Simon wondered what would happen if the children themselves reflected on their learning in different curriculum areas, writing their comments on the report pro-forma. The teachers could then pick up the threads of the learning conversation begun by each child and respond with their own thoughts. He shared this idea with Alison and, after discussing it and agreeing that it was workable, they opened it up for discussion at a staff meeting, inviting staff to think about if and how they might try the idea out.

Through this discussion, the staff team elaborated the approach together. The possibility emerged of setting up a buddy system, with older children paired with younger children to help them to reflect on their learning and record their ideas electronically onto the report. Alison suggested that teachers of the younger children could provide a prompt sheet for the older children, to support their discussions, with suggestions for suitable questions. Parents would be informed of curriculum content through a separate summary sheet appended to the reports, leaving people free to focus on the detail of children's learning in each area. Cheryl, the teacher of the 5- and 6-year-olds, supported the new approach, because she believed that what individual children thought about their learning was an excellent starting point for her own reflections. She bought folders for her children to use for storing their comments and as a way of demonstrating the value of their thoughts about their learning.

Another leadership strategy, recorded in Chapter 2, was promoting and resourcing worthwhile curriculum experiences. Substantial resources of time and money were invested in visits from artists and writers, in museum visits and trips to the theatre. Further examples have been described in detail in Chapter 3. From a leadership perspective, these various initiatives were worth every minute and every penny. As well as creating opportunities for children to learn from high-quality, open-ended, authentic experiences, they generated a lot of interest and sparked many conversations about learning across the teaching team; these conversations, as we have noted, were not concerned with levels or standards, but with children's capacity for learning. The initiatives communicated important messages about the kinds of experiences that make for enthusiastic, motivated learners while leaving colleagues free to assimilate these messages into their practice, without pressure, in their own way. Teaching staff also had the chance to see children in a different light, and to be impressed and surprised by the children's responses. All these experiences contributed to strengthening their trust in all children's powers as learners. As their trust grew, they increasingly distanced themselves from the use of 'ability' labels, which had been taken for granted in the frameworks for planning and teaching that they had been expected to use while the school was in special measures.

Connecting with the wider community of ideas and practices

The leadership team also played an important role in facilitating connections between the community of the school and the wider community of ideas and practices beyond the school. These connections were vital because they ensured that the whole staff, including the leadership team, were constantly exposed to fresh thinking, and regularly had the opportunity to exchange ideas and articulate their thinking in conversation with wider professional groups. Important sources of ideas and inspiration came in the form of books, articles and chapters to read. Alison wanted people's thinking to be nourished by the heritage of the ideas on which they were building. For example, at the end of the autumn term in 2006, Alison gave all members of the teaching team, 'as a Christmas treat!', a copy of a provocative piece by Professor Eliot Eisner, given as the John Dewey lecture for 2002, at Stanford University. Under the title 'What can education learn from the arts about the practice of education?' Eisner calls for the creation of a whole new culture of schooling to replace the technicized cognitive culture that he sees as dominant in contemporary education. In the closing passages, he identifies the key characteristics of this other way of thinking about the purposes and outcomes of schooling. He describes an educational culture that has:

> . . . a greater focus on becoming than on being, places more value on the imaginative than on the factual, assigns greater priority to valuing than to measuring, and regards the quality of the journey as more educationally significant than the speed at which the destination is reached. I am talking about a new vision of what education might become and what schools are for.
>
> (Eisner 2004: 10)

It is not difficult to see parallels between Eisner's vision and the possibilities beginning to open up at Wroxham. Alison herself said that she chose this article because she had personally been inspired by it, and thought that it might be enticing or challenging for colleagues, or 'spark a question'.

Just before Alison was due to open up discussion with staff and governors about the *Creating Learning without Limits* research project, based at the University of Cambridge, and invite their support and involvement, she gave out a copy of an article by the education researcher Boaler, presenting challenging yet compelling evidence that ability-grouping practices reproduce social class inequalities and, in the words of one ex-student, create 'psychological prisons' that 'break ambition' and 'almost formally label kids as stupid'. Boaler argues that:

> Children develop at different rates, and they reveal different interests, strengths and dispositions at various stages of their development. One of the most important goals of schools is to provide stimulating environments for all children; environments in which children's interest can be peaked and nurtured, with teachers who are ready to recognize, cultivate and develop the potential that children show at different times and in different areas. It is difficult to support [children's] development and nurture their potential if they are placed into a low group at a very early age, told that they are achieving at lower levels than others, given less challenging and interesting work, taught by less qualified and experienced teachers, and separated from peers who would stimulate their thinking.
>
> (Boaler 2005: 135)

Alison explained that she wanted people to have had a chance to engage with some of the important ideas, history and research that lay behind the study to be undertaken at Wroxham. During her two-plus years of headship, she had not held any formal discussions with the teaching team as a whole about ability labelling and grouping, although she had shared her thinking with individual colleagues when the topic arose in conversation. There had been no leadership directive to move away from ability-based practices, although most staff had begun to do so, as we have noted. As with the Eisner article, the paper was distributed and people were trusted to read and make sense of it in their own time and in their own ways. There was no check that it had been read, and no formal follow-up discussion attempting to reach or impose consensus about the messages it contained.

By encouraging contacts with the wider community of ideas, either directly through participation in networks, seminars or courses, or indirectly through carefully chosen readings and research, the leadership team made it clear that they expected and desired that colleagues should feel free to learn from other people, and not just from within the Wroxham community. Not only was there no obligation to comply with officially sanctioned 'best practice', but equally there was no pressure towards uniformity or desire to impose a 'Wroxham way'. The aim was to help people to find the richest possible nourishment for their learning, to inspire them to move beyond their existing thinking through exchanging ideas with other professionals who shared similar professional values and engaging with challenging ideas of key thinkers and researchers.

The stable environment

Enacting the leadership role, through these various strategies, with a sustained focus on children's learning, communicated unequivocal messages about leadership priorities. People saw and experienced for themselves how Alison was choosing to use her time and therefore were left in no doubt about what she most valued. Less visible perhaps was another important area of leadership activity, which created the time, space and energy for the whole staff group to sustain their focus on children's learning. Alison talked about the need to create a 'stable environment' for staff, where their safety was guaranteed. Within this secure environment, people could focus, undistracted and unpressurized, on the core purpose of the school.

For the staff team

For staff, the stable environment had three key features. First, they could trust in the smooth running of the school in the knowledge that efficient systems were in place. Colleagues knew that if they asked for something to be done, it would be taken care of without the need for them to chase it up. Secondly, they were shielded from unnecessary pressures and expectations because the leadership team filtered incoming non-statutory initiatives, ensuring that demands from outside were made manageable and could be taken up in a way that added fresh interest and impetus to work in progress. Time and space were created for the teaching teams to focus on learning. They were protected from pressure to adopt practices that might detract from work that they were already doing. For example, the account of the invention of Wroxham radio (in Chapter 2) shows how a pack of materials designed to be used for a series of staff meetings on speaking and listening was not used as intended but was instead opened up for critical discussion across the staff group. People were encouraged to respond creatively, taking into account what they were already doing to foster speaking and listening.

Thirdly, and most importantly, the stable environment provided a psychologically safe space, in which people knew that they were respected and valued, diversity of ideas and practices was welcomed and celebrated and staff knew support would always be available if they needed it. Part of this sense of security came from the school-wide mentoring system which ensured that *every* member of staff, including administrators, cleaning and kitchen staff, teaching assistants and the headteacher herself had someone to turn to, in complete confidence, to talk to about any issue arising in their work. In Chapter 4, we saw how important to Sophie was the support that Jo, her mentor, gave her when she was developing her eventually successful approach with her challenging class. Jo helped her to maintain perspective on what she and the class had already achieved, when her confidence in the progress they had made together suddenly plummeted. The mentoring system helped strengthen and sustain feelings of empathy, mutual recognition and collective responsibility across the staff team as a whole. They were all paired with someone who they knew was committed to empathizing with their perspective and understanding any concerns from their point of view. Mutual recognition and a sense of being valued by the collective were also fostered through the sharing and celebration of achievements. The successes and insights arising from activities such as Jo's Victorian bottles project and Martyn's Robin Hood Day were shared and celebrated within the community, becoming occasions for reassurance, encouragement and mutual appreciation, as well as learning, for the whole team.

Consistency was another element of the safety net. As people became aware of the principles that guided Alison's vision, they learned that they could trust that her actions would be in line with these principles. The principles not only ran through visible, school-wide, formal structures such as those we described in Chapter 2, but also permeated countless informal, moment by moment, ordinary, everyday activities and interactions. For example, messages regarding the equal value of every member of the school community – the principle of the 'ethic of everybody' as we described it in Chapter 1 – were communicated in many small but significant ways: the previous headteacher's designated parking space was converted into a parking bay for disabled visitors; a decision was taken that teaching staff and visitors should take their place in the queue for lunch along with the children, much to the consternation of a visiting inspector.

From the earliest days of her headship, Alison also worked to build a collective approach to behaviour issues that was both supportive of staff *and* consistent with her principles. It was important to ensure that people felt supported when they had concerns about behaviour (of children or other adults), since these could so easily and damagingly sap energy, confidence and morale. In Chapter 4 we showed how listening to everybody involved and trying to understand their subjective experience were crucial. Alison's default approach was to avoid complaint and blame, and instead to seek out creative solutions that enabled everybody to learn from the situation. But maintaining stability was also paramount, so when necessary Alison stepped in herself to give active support; she was also prepared to engage additional teaching assistants to ensure collective safety and aid staff in maintaining a positive approach.

On very rare occasions, too, there were times when Alison knew she just had to draw a line. Though it was hardly ever necessary, it was important for everybody to know that it could happen. Part of what gave people their sense of security – within the stable environment – was the knowledge that Alison would step in and take decisive action, if any individual member of staff consistently acted in ways that contravened the fundamental values and well-being of the community.

For the leadership team

A stable environment was also a prerequisite for the leadership team to have time and space to undertake the work that we have described in the first part of this chapter. The smooth management of the school through efficient systems and rigorous paperwork was one way of creating time. Alison understood that she could not accomplish the task of managing the school alone; her leadership depended on her capacity to delegate tasks with complete trust in the team around her. 'I don't need to do their job for them,' she said, 'It's about building a team so that everybody helps everybody else.' This trust in her team meant that Alison could avoid spending time and energy on anything that she considered headteachers need not do, things that would absorb substantial time away from her core focus on learning. Having appointed skilled and experienced people to take care of routine essentials – a highly qualified business manager to take care of financial matters and oversee school administration, and an experienced site manager to ensure high-quality maintenance of the premises – she had complete trust in their ability to carry out their designated responsibilities.

Sharing the running of the school with a trusted team meant that Alison was free to spend her time concentrating on teaching and learning. Being guided by principles, with clear priorities, helped Alison to resist pressures to spend time on administrative activities that she judged to be of limited value in promoting learning. For example, she believed that the current practice of regularly using computer software packages to collect and analyse data about children's levels of achievement was often a time-consuming distraction:

> . . . the emphasis is all in the wrong place, because you know who the children are who you are concerned about . . . The most important thing is, what are you going to do about it? How are you going to work with those children? How are you going to enable your staff? . . . How can you unlock the mystery of their learning so that they can make the next steps? The energy needs to be put into how we can improve

the learning for this child. What can we do collectively as a school, as a team, working with that child?

Fending off time-consuming and often irrelevant external pressures was more problematic when these took the form of external directives that were fundamentally opposed to everything that Alison believed in and stood for. The requirement for each school to draw up a register of supposedly 'gifted and talented' children presented one such challenge. How should she respond? Put down on paper some words that she considered meaningless, and in doing so collude with these damaging ways of thinking about children's potential, just to get the issue off her desk? Or resist and court censure on the grounds that, in a democracy, moral considerations should take precedence over flawed policy?

Alison faced many such complex dilemmas over the period of the research. She commented that she drew courage, inspiration and support from literature, research and from the wider community of educators beyond the school who shared similar core values, to help her work out how to respond in each case. Creating time and space for her own learning was an important precondition for enabling her to support the learning of the whole team. It was just as important for her, as for her colleagues, to be continually exposed to and engage with important educational ideas, both old and new. Alison was constantly searching for ideas that would help to sustain and nourish her belief that a more humane and empowering approach to education was possible and strengthen her efforts to realize it in practice. She did not look for nourishment or challenging new ideas in the recommendations and guidance contained in national policy documents. Instead she searched out books and articles by thoughtful, inspirational writers, took part in professional networks and attended carefully chosen conferences and seminars to stimulate and challenge her thinking; as well, she fostered many contacts with educators and researchers working in institutions of higher education in order to join with them in ongoing dialogue and exchange of ideas. Included in these, of course, were the regular conversations with the Cambridge-based research team during our study of Wroxham. Though sustaining these contacts required a significant investment of time, this investment was amply rewarded. Alison was able continually to enrich the repertoire of possibilities and alternative ways of thinking on which she could draw in supporting and stimulating the thinking of her colleagues as opportunities arose. She also drew from them courage and confidence to hold on to her principles, especially in meeting new challenges.

Building a community of powerful professional learners

Looking back at the range of leadership activities described in the first part of this chapter, we can see how the principles of co-agency, trust and everybody that Alison brought with her to Wroxham (described in Chapter 1) have come to be embodied in strategies for supporting staff learning. We can see how they reflect and promote her perception of colleagues as active thinkers and learners in their own right, who can and must do their own thinking if worthwhile learning is to take place. We can appreciate how she managed to offer significant support of a kind that was consistent with a deep trust in people's professionalism, with trust in their capacity to learn without being told what to do. We can also see how, by encouraging collaboration and mutual support, she created conditions for people to share expertise, to learn from and with one another and value each other's contributions. Although for much of the time Alison was responding intuitively to situations and opportunities as they arose, she also consciously used these principles to monitor and reflect on her developing approach. Sometimes, too, she drew on the principles explicitly and used them in conversations with colleagues to help in making choices between alternative courses of action.

Less formally articulated, however, were the underlying purposes that the leadership strategies were working towards. Although these purposes were only made explicit gradually through the research process, we now understand that, embedded in the strategies, there is a coherent view of the particular *dispositions* that the leadership strategies were seeking to cultivate, across the whole staff team. By cultivating these, the aim was to create a community of powerful learners, dedicated to a particular kind of professional learning, and supported by the energy of the collective. The sustained use of the various leadership strategies, within the context of a stable environment, created the conditions for colleagues to build and strengthen seven key dispositions, while also reducing and minimizing states of mind that inhibit learning; these dispositions and states of mind are summarized in Table 5.1.

A first key disposition being cultivated was *openness*. This includes openness to new ideas and possibilities and to new opportunities and experiences; a willingness to learn from and be receptive to the ideas of everybody within the community; openness to what children might learn, separately and together, from their engagement in learning experiences, rather than from prespecified outcomes; openness of mind about children's learning capacity, not predetermining or placing any sort of ceiling on what anyone might do, learn or accomplish; openness to surprise and to previously unthought-of possibilities. Openness means giving up the belief that there is one right way or a ready-made solution, if only it could be found, giving up the notion of learning as progress towards perfection. It means accepting instead that learning is open-ended, and ever-continuing. However much anyone knows, there is always more to learn.

A second disposition was *questioning*. Questioning means restlessly searching for better ways of doing things. It means not taking the status quo

Table 5.1 Dispositions that increase capacity for professional learning

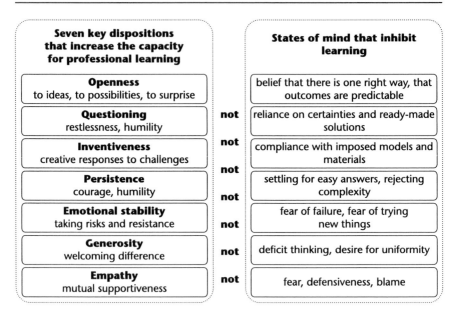

Seven key dispositions that increase the capacity for professional learning		States of mind that inhibit learning
Openness to ideas, to possibilities, to surprise		belief that there is one right way, that outcomes are predictable
Questioning restlessness, humility	not	reliance on certainties and ready-made solutions
Inventiveness creative responses to challenges	not	compliance with imposed models and materials
Persistence courage, humility	not	settling for easy answers, rejecting complexity
Emotional stability taking risks and resistance	not	fear of failure, fear of trying new things
Generosity welcoming difference	not	deficit thinking, desire for uniformity
Empathy mutual supportiveness	not	fear, defensiveness, blame

for granted, but continually asking 'Does it have to be like this?' 'Is there a better way?' 'What else can I do'? Questioning is driven by a belief that change is possible, and it *makes* change possible, by generating new ideas and insights that point towards new possibilities for practice. The disposition of questioning is the opposite of complacency; it is a form of humility, the default mode of people who know that they do not have all the answers, that they must keep learning themselves in order to do their best for children. Questioning increases people's sense of power and agency. At Wroxham, as we have seen, asking questions about practice, about children's learning, about themselves as teachers, and about the relationship between these, was one way by which members of the teaching team stayed in control and shaped the path and pace of their own learning, rather than following someone's lead, or an agenda determined by others. Within the team, asking questions was recognized as a mark of commitment and expertise, not of inexperience. The more powerful, probing and insightful the questions, the better stimulus they provided for the growth of understanding. Through sharing each other's questions and tussling with them together, colleagues helped to build a culture in which the act of questioning was constantly validated and strengthened.

Questioning was intimately bound up with *inventiveness*. Inventiveness involves the desire and capacity to imagine and do something new. If a solution cannot be found within existing repertoires, then inventiveness is needed to come up with an idea that offers a way forward. At Wroxham, inventiveness was needed to create new ways of thinking and learning to replace ability-based thinking and practices; it was needed to find ways to meld together National Curriculum programmes of study with children's own ideas about what they wanted to do and learn, and what made sense to them; it was needed to enrich and enliven the curriculum with more engaging, authentic learning opportunities. Wroxham teaching staff had complete licence, indeed active leadership encouragement, to depart as they saw fit from non-statutory frameworks, downloaded lesson plans and ready-made packs of materials. They were encouraged to think, act and make choices in the interests of children, to take risks in trying out new ideas. But inventiveness needs to go hand in hand with questioning, to help in evaluating learning and adapting and refining new approaches. *Persistence* is also essential. Significant new ideas and worthwhile innovations often require persistent thought, sustained effort and progressive refinement before they become established and embedded. It is important not to shy away from complexity or to give up on promising new possibilities prematurely. Most importantly, persistence is also about not giving up on people, keeping up efforts in the belief that desired changes are always possible, even if the key has not yet been found. As does questioning, persistence goes hand in hand with the personal qualities of courage and humility. Persistence reflects awareness that worthwhile learning necessarily involves struggle, yet acknowledges that to struggle is positive, especially when engaged in with others offering mutual support, and when struggling for something believed in, rather than struggling *against* something imposed from outside.

Emotional stability is a precondition for enabling openness, questioning, inventiveness and persistence to flourish. It is grounded in a sense of acceptance, in each person's sense of being valued and making a unique contribution to the collective. Emotional stability is the state of mind that enables risk taking; if people feel safe and secure, they are better able to rely on their own judgement; they are also better able to hold firm to what they believe in, and resist pressure to adopt ways of thinking or practices that they do not fully understand or agree with. Emotional stability generates the strength to resist popular notions of ability and the models of 'good practice' that embody them. It releases the energy and resilience needed to cope with the challenging approach to teaching and learning being fostered within the whole staff group.

A further disposition being cultivated was *generosity*. Generosity is an expression of trust in everybody's capacity to learn; it implies an open acceptance of everybody. Generosity embraces diversity as an important resource for the learning of the whole community; everybody has a rightful place within the collective, so there is a collective responsibility to take action if necessary to enable everybody to belong more fully, to be accepted and to make a contribution. Generosity entails engaging with others – whether colleagues, children or parents – in an open, accepting, non-defensive way. Responding to others in a spirit of generosity is the direct opposite of acting in a spirit of blame or complaint. Generosity is the human face of persistence. It entails believing the best of people and approaching them with hope and optimism, believing that things will improve as a result of one's efforts. Generosity creates human space within which more considered thought can be given to alternative courses of action before agreement is reached about ways forward that will best serve the interests of everybody.

Finally, the disposition of *empathy* was being fostered within the staff team in their dealings with one another, with other staff, parents and children. Empathy is essentially about listening to others and attempting to understand the world through their eyes. Empathy helps teaching staff to understand what it is that a child does not understand, when difficulties arise, and so to respond in ways that engage more closely with the child's thinking. At Wroxham, as we saw in Chapter 4, it is a key quality of the relationships that staff were working to build with children, an important source of insight and understanding and a way of more fully knowing the children. Nurtured within the staff team, empathy drives out isolation and fear; when coupled with mutual supportiveness, it means that all responsibilities are shared within the collective, so that no one need ever feel isolated or alone, no one need feel embarrassment or shame to seek help if they are experiencing difficulties.

Having looked in detail at the dispositions the leadership strategies were working towards, we can better appreciate the basis for Alison's confidence, from the outset, that if colleagues were given freedom to develop their practice in their own time and in their own ways, with appropriate support, this would lead to developments that were compatible with the kind of school she wanted to create. If these dispositions were continually enacted, nurtured and strengthened across the whole teaching team, they would not only strengthen people's agency as autonomous learners in their own right, but would lead to a particular kind of professional learning: the kind of learning that people can only do for themselves, learning that is both intellectually and emotionally challenging, that happens slowly over time and involves struggle. While deeply personal, it is also essentially social and collaborative. When people learn together, the power of the collective strengthens the learning capacity of each individual; more can be achieved together than any one of them could achieve alone.

Looking back at the developments described in earlier chapters of the book reveals the dispositions reflected in teachers' accounts of their work, in their thinking and their developing practice. Martyn's Robin Hood Day is not simply a story about inspiring writing, but, more importantly, a story about responding to a concern about children's motivation with generosity and inventiveness. Cheryl's experience of trying new ways of working with her class is a story that demonstrates the significance of emotional stability: her openness to new ideas was buttressed by her determination to probe and question the impact on each and every child in her class; she resisted pressure from the collective to move in a particular direction before she had seen for herself what difference it would make and arrived at her own conclusions. Darrelle's use of empathy in her relationships with children not only communicated vital personal recognition and worth but also enabled her to lift limits on learning that might not otherwise have come to her attention. Jo's account of her research with her Year 5 class on a shared language for learning shows what can be achieved when openness to the ideas of others includes inviting children to work in partnership with a teacher to develop understanding and practice together. All seven dispositions are revealed in Sophie's work to build a successful approach with her challenging class congruent with the kind of teacher she wanted to be. Simon's determination to ask questions constantly of his practice reflects a commitment to taking nothing for granted. He questioned not just how he could do things better but *why* he was doing what he was doing. Were children being given too much choice? Did differentiation through choice of task really change anything fundamental? Openness, questioning, persistence and inventiveness are evident in every teacher's approach to extending choices of levels of work and encouraging collaborative learning; because they believed in what they were striving for, they kept working at it, each in their own ways, supporting and sustaining one another through sharing ideas and practices.

While we cannot know the extent to which people were already disposed to think and behave in these ways, in these examples the dispositions that Alison was seeking to cultivate can be clearly seen in action. We are not suggesting that leadership work was directed toward creating dispositions that might not otherwise have existed; rather the purpose was to strengthen these particular dispositions within the professional community and to reduce or minimize others. One important way in which this was done, as the examples in this chapter show, was by Alison enacting and modelling these dispositions herself in her interactions with colleagues and in relation to her own learning. Her openness to other people's thinking and her reluctance to impose her ideas were acknowledged again and again by colleagues as they expressed appreciation of being able to pursue their own agenda for development, in their own way. Her colleague, Darrelle, noted and valued her stability: 'She's not threatened by what we do. She's quite happy to be challenged, and if she thinks that the challenge is correct and she's wrong, then she'll change.' Martyn commented, in a moment of exhilaration, that there were no limits to what teachers could do at Wroxham. But in fact there *were* limits, as Alison herself stressed. While diversity and idiosyncrasy were welcomed, even actively encouraged within the teaching team, the freedom that colleagues enjoyed and appreciated was a principled freedom. Anything was possible as long as it was consistent with the framework of principles, increasingly understood and shared by staff, that was guiding whole-school development.

Engaging everybody in the school-wide culture of learning

In this chapter, so far, we have explored the leadership role in working with the staff team to create conditions for the growth of a school-wide culture of learning. We have shown that it entails building a powerful community of professional learners who are committed to and collectively enact particular dispositions, every day, in relationships with each other, with children, with parents, with all members of the school community; it entails drawing on the power of the group to take pride in, recognize, sustain and nurture these dispositions as integral to their collective, professional identity. 'Putting learning first' means giving priority to actions and use of resources that foster the development of the seven dispositions and actively working to reduce and minimize states of mind that undermine their development.

As noted earlier, however, when Alison spoke of the need to develop a school-wide culture of learning, she was not just talking about the learning of teaching staff but of *everybody* in the school community. Earlier chapters showed some of the ways in which other people – children, of course, parents and carers, support staff, school governors – were drawn in and encouraged to become active participants in the school-wide culture of learning. Some of the early developments discussed in Chapter 2 not only laid important foundations for staff learning; they were also designed to transform children's sense of belonging, their sense of participation in school life and capacity to influence their experiences of learning. The school-wide circle group meetings, for instance, signalled to children that everybody had a rightful place in the community and that everybody would be listened to. Leadership of these meetings by Year 6 children laid foundations for profound changes in the balance of power and relationships; it also sent important messages to all children about their capacity to exercise leadership responsibilities. Learning review meetings enabled children to be active participants in discussions about their learning, to shape the course of the conversation and contribute to decisions about the next steps to be taken. All the examples of developments in practice described in Chapter 3 reflect further efforts on the part of the teaching team to increase children's opportunities to exercise control and have a say in their own learning. Revisiting the themes of Chapter 4, with the dispositions in mind, illuminates the growth of *ways of being* with children that are profoundly different from traditional teacher-pupil relationships. Children's participation in the school-wide culture of learning naturally increased in parallel with the growth of the dispositions that stimulated and increased staff learning.

Parents were increasingly drawn into the school-wide culture of learning partly as a result of sharing the enthusiasms of their children and partly through important new structures such as the learning review meetings. In these meetings parents were welcomed as co-educators, not simply as people to be informed about their children's progress in school. Parents' deep knowledge and understanding of their children were used as resources, alongside those of the teacher, to discuss the issues that the child brought to the meeting. Much effort was also put into breaking down barriers, so that parents felt comfortable coming into school and, if they were able to make an active contribution, to find ways of involving them that drew on their personal knowledge and skills. Parents to whom we spoke during the period of the research expressed appreciation of how welcome they felt in the school, how easy it was to talk to teaching staff and to Alison, and how any concerns they had were always listened to. They were able to articulate clearly their sense of what the school stood for, and their understanding of why staff chose not to label and group children by ability, as we saw in Chapter 4. They strongly supported the imaginative approaches to curriculum being developed in the school, and commended the emphasis on children learning to care for one another, to work together as a team and help one another. As they talked about the key characteristics of the school, it was clear that one reason why they valued the Wroxham approach so highly was because their priorities for their children were not concerned with standards, achievement, and academic goals; they wanted their children to develop a thirst for learning, to feel happy about themselves, to be rounded individuals and good members of the community. Their sense of how they and their children were treated led to a desire, even a sense of moral obligation, to become more involved. One parent commented, 'They make you feel important, and your child important, so you have to contribute to the school as well.'

This parent's comment went right to the very heart of the matter. Making people 'feel important' was far more than just fine words. People *were* important, crucially important, because the power of the collective to bring about change depended upon everybody's contribution. 'It's all about co-agency,' Alison said. Her ability to use her power as a leader to move the school in the direction of her vision was conditional upon the extent to which all members of the school community used *their* power, individually and collectively, to contribute to those developments. This was why a school-wide culture of learning was so essential and why Alison devoted her energies to developing it so determinedly.

The moral imperative

There is one last piece of the jigsaw, however, that we need to put in place, perhaps the most important of all, if we are to give a full picture of how developments at Wroxham were being created and sustained. As we noted in our discussion of persistence, the struggles that worthwhile learning necessarily entails are positive when they are undertaken in order to move towards something that people believe is worth striving for. This sense of moral purpose – the contribution that people believe they can make to creating a better world – comes from deep-rooted values; it gives rise to a passion that drives people on and makes the struggle not just worthwhile but even exhilarating. Reflecting on what she had learned from the research, Alison explained that she now understands more fully that what sustains people and drives them on is principally *passion*. Passion arises when one's vision of a better future is coupled with a sense of one's own power to make it happen. In her leadership work with the teaching team, Alison was not just fostering particular dispositions, she was fostering a shared sense of what they were all learning *for*, what they were striving together to create: a school environment in which everybody's learning could flourish, free from the damaging effects of ability labels and ability-focused practices. By nurturing the seven dispositions, she was enabling the teaching team to discover progressively their own power to contribute to this shared moral purpose.

So the ultimate test of any strategy, for Alison, was whether it helped to strengthen people's sense of passionate endeavour, if it helped to increase their sense of their own agency, their ability to imagine and bring about worthwhile changes through their own efforts. As members of the Wroxham team progressively embraced a more open view of children's learning capacity, and as their confidence in their own agency increased, so they became autonomous, self-sustaining learners in their own right. Their ongoing study of children's learning provided an open-ended agenda for change and improvement; the school-wide culture of learning helped to nurture and sustain their passion through the power of the collective, cultivating shared energy and hope within the team. And this energy, passion and hope were harnessed to the very big transformative idea at the heart of the changes that were coming about in the school. As this work continued – and continues – the moral purpose that drives the teaching staff at Wroxham becomes less and less a remote or unattainable aspiration. It becomes instilled with immediacy; it becomes rooted in their everyday actions and encounters. Indeed, as Harriet Cuffaro argues, in an extended account of how the educational philosophy of John Dewey has enduring significance, and how she learned to apply his principles in her own practice, teachers who are committed to coherence and integrity in their work come to understand that 'teaching is a way of being who we are, and a place where in our actions we make manifest what we believe and value' (Cuffaro 1995: 98). The work of teachers *is* the site where their moral purpose is enacted.

6 The power of collective action

We have now reached the point in our story where we review what we have learned from the Wroxham community about how to build a learning environment that is safe, humane, enabling and equitable for everybody, a place free from the limiting effects of ability labels and practices. From the outset, Alison argued that the purposes and principles that were found to guide individual teachers' classroom decision making in the earlier study apply just as much to adult learning as to children's learning. The model of classroom pedagogy could not be fully effective for children unless the same purposes and principles were also being applied to support the learning of staff. We now know what becomes possible when a shared trust in children's learning capacity and awareness of teachers' professional power are embedded in and inspire developments on a school-wide basis. Transforming the learning capacity of teaching staff is *the* condition for transforming the learning capacity of children. In this chapter we consider how the power of leadership, the power of the collective and the passion of individual teachers each make their contribution to creating conditions in which professional learning can flourish. We distil the distinctive features of school improvement at Wroxham and how these contrast with the approach sponsored by the standards agenda. We draw out the relevance and applicability of our findings for individual teachers, school leaders, teacher education providers, and policy makers. We then consider what lies ahead and the scope for further research.

The power to transform learning capacity

In Chapter 1, we explained briefly how our study of The Wroxham School built on the findings of the first project, published in *Learning without Limits* (Hart *et al.* 2004). We noted that this study focused solely on what individual teachers, working in a variety of different contexts, had the power to do in their own classrooms to develop practices that were consistent with their principled rejection of ability labelling and ability-focused practices. They were strongly aware, however, of the limits to what they could do in isolation; there were many more possibilities for development that could only be pursued if people were working together towards a common vision, and if there was strong leadership support for such developments. Alison's appointment to the headship at Wroxham created an exciting opportunity to explore these wider possibilities.

Of course, when Alison arrived at Wroxham, the staff did not yet know of their headteacher's vision and her guiding purposes and principles. Our study deliberately focused on the school as it developed; we wanted to find out how Alison would communicate her ideas to her colleagues and how they would take up the invitation to work together to build a school in which every child's learning could flourish. In the early days of her headship, she did not directly confront ideas about ability or attempt to persuade people, through argument and evidence, to share her views about the damage that ability-focused practices can do. Instead, she set up structures and provided experiences that helped to nurture colleagues' trust in every child's capacity to learn, as we saw in Chapter 2; she then worked systematically, as we showed in Chapter 5, to build colleagues' sense of their power to transform children's learning capacity through the everyday choices and decisions they make in their classroom practice. The process of school development at Wroxham, as we now understand it, is summarized in Figure 6.1.

Through our study of the leadership role, in Chapter 5, we have developed important new insights into what can be done to increase teachers' power to make transforming choices in three key areas: through the work of leadership, through the work of the staff collective and through the endeavours of individual teachers. In the first part of this chapter we summarize what we have learnt about the possibilities presented by each of these areas and the contribution they make to the development of teachers' powers.

The work of leadership

From the first *Learning without Limits* study, we learned that teachers' power to increase children's learning capacity depends on their understanding of the interplay between external forces and internal states of mind, both of which affect children's capacity to learn, and on their awareness of the extent to which both are susceptible to change by their own choices and actions in the present (see Figure 6.2). In the use of this power, teachers continually reflect on their choices, deepening their understanding of the factors that impinge on learning capacity, and constantly working to expand it.

Our study of Wroxham has shown how much school leaders can do to strengthen individual teachers' power through their own choices and actions.

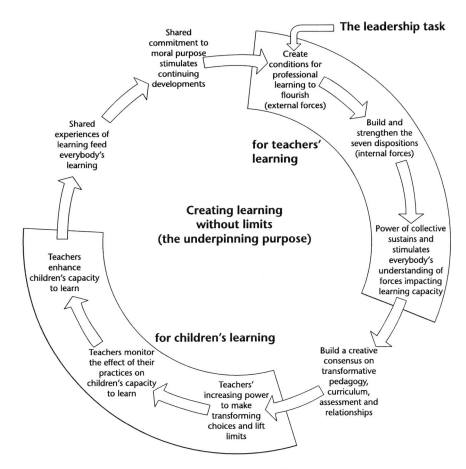

Figure 6.1 Creating learning without limits: a model of school development

Careful judgement is needed, week in and week out, in deciding what to do and what not to do in creating conditions for professional learning to flourish. We now understand that this task has two key dimensions, which parallel the two sets of forces in Figure 6.2. On the one hand, it entails creating *external* conditions that support and stimulate learning for each member of the team individually and for everybody collectively. On the other hand, it entails nurturing the *internal* dispositions that teachers need if they are to do the kind of learning upon which building a school dedicated to learning without limits depends.

In Chapter 5 we explored in detail the leadership role in creating the external conditions – the structures and strategies that support and stimulate professional learning and the features of the stable environment that free

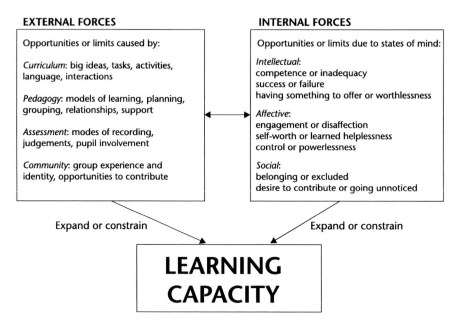

Figure 6.2 Forces affecting learning capacity

Source: Adapted from Hart *et al.* (2004).

teaching staff to focus on learning. We can now see that these were deeply principled actions, reflecting the *Learning without Limits* principles outlined in Chapter 1. The analysis confirms Alison's conviction that these principles do also apply to the learning of staff, and provides detailed insight into exactly *how* these principles can be translated into practice to support staff learning. Table 6.1 shows how the leadership strategies we examined in detail in Chapter 5, and summarized in the continuum shown in Figure 5.1, can be seen to be wholly congruent with the key pedagogical principles of co-agency, everybody and trust.

New to this study is the articulation of *internal* conditions necessary for powerful professional learning to flourish. The same strategies that build the external conditions for professional learning also cultivate particular internal dispositions – ways of being, ways of engaging with others and with experience – that enable people to become autonomous, self-sustaining learners in their own right. Although the seven dispositions described in Chapter 5 were identified specifically through our study of what was happening at Wroxham, it is not difficult to find accounts of similar qualities of mind in other texts, by a whole variety of educational writers, researchers and theorists. Stenhouse (1975), for example, in a discussion of the role of the teacher in 'the betterment of schools',

Table 6.1   Principles governing leadership strategies

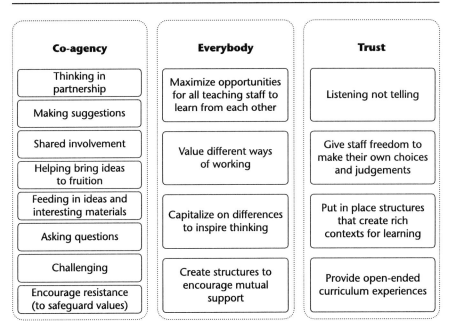

places responsibility for this task firmly in the hands – and minds – of teachers. One characteristic of this role is 'the commitment to systematic *questioning* of one's own teaching as a basis for development.' He goes on to add as 'highly desirable' the 'readiness to allow other teachers to observe one's work . . . and to discuss it with them on an *open* and honest basis' (p. 144, italics added). In a later work, Stenhouse expands on the desirable qualities of the researcher, distinguishing the teacher as 'a conscious artist', practising the art of teaching. This is no idle metaphor, as he makes clear: 'If my words are inadequate, look at the sketchbook of a good artist, a play in rehearsal, a jazz quartet working together. That, I am arguing, is what good teaching looks like' (1985: 97). He may not use the very term *inventiveness*, but his words are clearly intended to emphasize the quality we have called by that name, the necessity of creativity in teaching, the essential capacity to imagine and enact new practices.

Another striking parallel can be found in the work of Susan Isaacs, who based her work as a teacher educator on her intensive observations of children. The strength of her observations, their lasting significance, lies in part in her highly developed capacity for what we have called *openness*. In her own words, in the introduction to *Social Development in Young Children*:

> I was not prepared to select . . . only such behaviour as pleased me, or as fitted into the general convention as to what little

> children should feel and talk about . . . I was just as ready to record and to study the less attractive aspects of their behaviour as the more pleasing, whatever my aims and preferences as their educator might be.
>
> (Isaacs 1933: 19)

And later in the same text she explains the reason for this position: 'I myself happen to be interested in *everything* that children do and feel' (p. 113, Isaacs' italics).

The importance of *emotional stability*, which we have described in terms of a sense of acceptance, safety and security, is explored in a challenging paper by Roger Harrison, first published in 1963, entitled 'Defences and the need to know'. He describes the universal human need to know, seen in the baby 'who begins to explore as soon as he or she can crawl', and equally in 'our continuing efforts to understand and master the world as adults'. The problem he identifies is that 'the need to know is the enemy of comfort, stability and a placid existence'; there is a continual struggle between the defences that protect our well-established conceptual systems, that give our lives stability and security, that keep our relations with others pleasant and satisfying, and 'our desires to increase our competence and understanding'. The nub of Harrison's argument is that 'the destruction of defences does not serve learning' – rather, it increases anxiety and insecurity. What then is to be done with the paradox that 'we cannot increase learning by destroying the defences that block it'?

Harrison's solution is vividly portrayed:

> What we can do is create situations where people will not need to stay behind their defences all the time. We can make it safe for them to sally forth from behind the moat, so to speak, secure in the knowledge that while they are exploring the countryside no one will sneak in and burn the castle.
>
> (Harrison [1963] 1995: 290)

In conclusion, Harrison describes the necessary qualities of adult relationships in which learning from one another is possible: 'relationships of mutual support, respect and trust' – a striking corroboration of the themes of Chapters 4 and 5.

People with the internal dispositions identified at Wroxham are well placed to do the kinds of thinking and learning that enable them to move beyond their existing understandings, recognize and lift limits and develop new possibilities for practice. As we show in Table 6.2, in the intellectual domain, the disposition of *openness* necessarily entails keeping an open mind, not prejudging what any child might achieve; *questioning* is needed to explore

Table 6.2 Building the dispositions characteristic of powerful autonomous learners

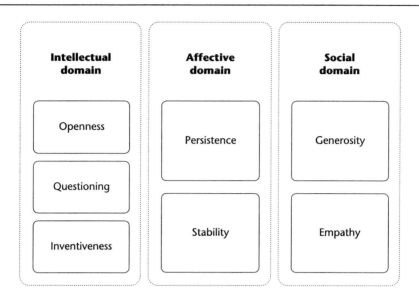

what is helping and hindering learning and what might be done differently to engage learners' powers more fully; *inventiveness* enables teachers to imagine and construct new practices to replace ability-based pedagogy. In the affective domain, *persistence* is needed to keep doors open, to continually search for ways of unlocking learning for children; *stability* is needed to hold firm to values and principles, while still being open to challenge. In the social domain, *generosity* is needed to appreciate and learn from diversity, rather than treating differences as deficits; and *empathy* entails understanding and relating to people in all their complexity and uniqueness, without recourse to reductive categories.

External conditions and internal dispositions work together to create powerful professional learners, so leadership support is at its most powerful when strategies take account of both dimensions, particularly when the energy of the collective is harnessed to support and stimulate everybody's learning.

The power of the collective

It was understood by the leadership at Wroxham that just as, in the classroom, children's learning capacity is deeply affected – for better or worse – by how the class functions as a group, so the learning capacity of each member of the teaching team is affected by the ethos of the staff group and how well people work together to sustain and inspire one another's learning. This is why so much emphasis was placed on creating conditions for the growth of a culture of learning, and especially on providing opportunities for people to work and learn together.

One important way in which the collective exerted a positive influence was by fostering a sense of shared professional identity. A collective pride was being cultivated within the team and *by* the team: pride in being a particular kind of teacher and in being a member of a group of powerful professional learners. Jo talked about the atmosphere of excitement among the staff that was so different from how it had been when they were in special measures. Wroxham had become a place where people were eager for dialogue, debate and reflection, a place of hope: 'Nobody says "Well that's it, I've had enough!".' The team played an important part in nurturing the dispositions that helped define this shared identity, by recognizing, valuing and celebrating these ways of being and learning in one another. For example, growing recognition of the value of openness and questioning rather than certainty meant that colleagues were able to draw reassurance and inspiration from each other's questions and struggles as well as from their successes. As a result, confidence and morale were boosted, and a 'can-do' attitude prevailed. Individuals took pride in their own choices and in working things out for themselves, spurred on by the recognition they received from the team. The sustaining power of the team gave individuals the confidence to take risks as they explored new possibilities. It both supported them in their endeavours, and generated ideas to help. This sustaining power also gave them strength to keep trying when complications arose or problems were encountered. In this way, the capacity of individual teachers to make choices in the interests of increasing children's learning capacity was enhanced by the power of the team.

In interview, members of staff sometimes wondered if this sense of shared identity was due to the particular individuals who happened to be teaching at Wroxham at the time. Would it still be there when staffing changed? Recent evidence shows that, despite a number of changes in staffing, the same sense of shared identity persists to the present day, several years after the research was carried out. At a staff meeting in 2011, people read short summaries of the seven dispositions outlined in Chapter 5 and were asked to comment on how meaningful they found them in relation to their own experience of teaching at Wroxham. The activity produced an excited buzz of recognition; staff agreed that the descriptions of the dispositions do capture something essential, and enduring, about what it is to be a teacher at Wroxham, about what people value in each other, and about the way that people live, work and learn together.

A second important way in which the collective supported the learning of individual teachers was through the emergence of a consensus about where to focus their efforts, in developing their practice, in order to increase children's learning capacity. As we described in Chapter 3, it became apparent that there was consensus on the single core purpose of enabling children to experience greater freedom and control over their learning. This was achieved through a broad range of interdependent, interlocking strategies, as illustrated in Figure 6.3. Though a selection of examples, rather than a comprehensive list, every item in this figure is derived from the data, and has been discussed in earlier chapters. In Chapter 3, we puzzled over how to reconcile this strong agreement within the whole team with the equally strong evidence that everybody valued, and experienced, the freedom to do their own thinking and find their own way. Clarifying the range of dispositions that were being fostered within the group helped us to appreciate more fully how the consensus was working to enable, not constrain, individual learning. The dispositions facilitate learning that is both individual and autonomous, *and* collective and interdependent. Openness combined with questioning, stability and inventiveness, for instance, makes for a dynamic mix. People were not simply following one another's lead, or the lead provided by more experienced members of the group. The consensus was a creative one; working around common themes meant that people could share ideas and

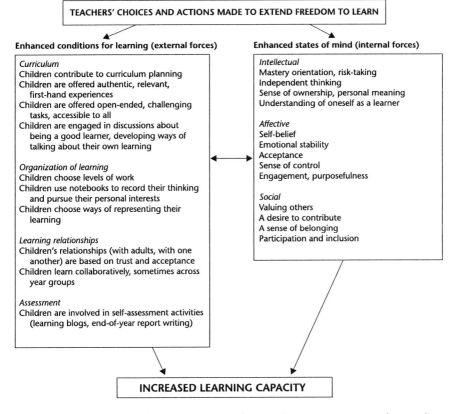

Figure 6.3 Transforming learning capacity: the creative consensus around extending freedom to learn

experiences, contribute to each other's thinking and learn from each other's practices, while still controlling and shaping the path of their own learning, for and with their particular class of children. Because everybody was 'on the same wave length', as Martyn put it, collaboration was especially productive, sparking ideas across the group, while leaving people free to develop their own distinctively individual practices. Each person's experiences, questions, new ideas, dilemmas and successful practices became resources for the whole group, while the resources of the group were made available to each individual to stimulate further thinking and developments. The creative consensus gave the group a coherent framework for ongoing shared enquiry to which everybody contributed and from which everybody could learn.

As we studied the workings of the consensus, we realized that it provided a further critically important answer to our question of what becomes possible, in creating learning without limits, when a whole-school staff work together towards common purposes, guided by common principles, rather than when individual teachers are acting alone. As well as supporting and sustaining staff learning, individually and collectively, the creative consensus also has significant and far-reaching implications for enhancing the learning capacity of children, not just in the immediate term but far into the future. It meant that children were able to experience consistency and coherence in these broad elements of curriculum and pedagogy across the whole school: for example, making choices, expressing their views, contributing to planning, learning collaboratively, understanding themselves as learners and assessing their own learning. This consistency made it possible for progress in all these areas, and the resulting impact on their learning capacity, to be sustained in the transition from one year group to the next, and further developed as they progressed through the school. It also strengthened children's power to be, and become, more active agents in their own learning. Understanding 'how we learn at Wroxham' put them in a position to take initiatives themselves, to offer to their teachers their own insights into what helps learning and so contribute themselves to the task of enhancing their own and their teachers' learning capacity.

The power of passion: being and becoming committed to learning without limits

In exploring what we have learned from our study of Wroxham, we have focused so far on how leadership support and the support of the collective can increase individual power to enhance children's learning capacity. It is important, though, not to underestimate the contribution of individual members of the teaching team, to recognize how much their individual initiative, courage and resourcefulness also contributed to school-wide developments. By the end of the research period, it was evident that people had become passionate advocates, individually, of the direction that the school was moving in; this commitment energized their individual power to increase children's learning capacity.

So what can we learn from them about what is involved in *becoming* committed to learning without limits? What have we learned about how people manage to resist the ideas of fixed ability, so pervasive in our culture, and discover their own power to transform learning capacity? Although the first *Learning without Limits* study did not allow us to explore these processes of becoming in detail, we learned from the nine teachers whose classrooms we studied that in most cases they had had direct personal experience of the damaging effects of ability labelling, of learning opportunities curtailed and hopes for the future demolished by judgements of fixed potential made about themselves, members of their family or friends. Some teachers had been shocked and inspired to work for change by seeing the effects of ability labelling on children during their professional lives. Their shared sense of the injustices bound up with these seemingly common-sense categories was profound.

Like the teachers in the first study, Wroxham teachers too came to reject fixed ability thinking and ability labelling through their own first-hand experiences. We found that, as in all aspects of whole-school development, there was no imposition of a 'right' way of thinking about children's learning capacity. Alison was mindful not to create inadvertently a culture of compliance or, worse, a climate of 'political correctness', where people avoided using ability labels because they knew these were frowned on, but nothing changed deep down in their thinking about children's powers as learners. People had time to chew over and express their doubts. Indeed, Simon himself articulated a similar concern over whether new approaches to differentiation were in fact just changing the labels.

In keeping with the principles of trust and co-agency, space was afforded for people's thinking to evolve in their own time and their own way. Alison trusted that, with the kinds of learning experiences on offer at Wroxham, her colleagues would come to their own understandings about the redundancy of ability labelling and the damage that it can do to everybody's thinking and learning. In earlier chapters we described new structures and experiences, new learning opportunities for teaching staff and for children, that revealed children's powers in a new light. In Chapter 5, we showed how the focus on children's learning tapped into people's deep-rooted commitment to doing their very best for children, how it prompted everyone to look closer at and think more about what children were doing and saying in response to classroom activities and so to build a richer understanding of children's learning, framed in ways that defied simplistic categorization. Conversations about children helped build a rich language for talking about learning in which ability labels had no place. Perhaps most significantly, the children themselves provided the evidence that challenged the concept of ability and made it redundant. A new member of staff who spent a day with the research team during the writing process said: 'The children feel invincible, as if there is no limit to what they can achieve.' The more closely people looked, the more they saw the children do; the more they learnt about what makes a difference, in the classroom environment, to children's capacity to learn, the more they discovered they could do themselves to support children's learning. A synergy between children's and teachers' learning emerged as people tried out new things, noticed how children responded, reflected on what to do next, adjusted their plans, saw the children becoming more enthusiastic, powerful learners, and expanded their sense of what was possible for all children.

Though the word 'transformability' was not used by any of the staff, and they made no explicit references to their power to 'transform learning capacity', understanding of these core ideas gradually became embedded in people's thinking and practices, as they worked out for themselves reasons to resist ability labelling based on their own understandings and values. Because this process was freely carried out, over an extended period of time, and was under each individual's control, the learning that resulted had deep personal significance. People expressed strong negative views about ability labelling and ability-based practices, and related how these changed perceptions carried over into their personal lives. They were able genuinely to commit to a shared vision of a school where children's learning could flourish free from the limits imposed by ability labels. They understood that what they were doing together was something indeed worth striving for. Their passion provided the constant impetus, the self-renewing sense of purpose, to do the learning that would enable them to play their full part in creating the kind of school to which they were now committed.

A distinctive approach to school improvement

We now move on to consider how the approach to school development that we have documented at Wroxham is different from the approach to improvement sponsored by national policy. Does our study provide convincing insight into a principled and practicable alternative approach, and if so, what are its defining features? We suggest that the Wroxham approach is profoundly different in a number of ways.

Intrinsic drive for change: a shared belief in something worth striving for

A first distinctive feature of the Wroxham approach is that the drive to improve is generated increasingly from *within*. The standards agenda relies on external pressure, for example in the form of externally imposed targets, competition between schools, league tables, performance management, performance-related pay and grading of schools through regular inspections. If 'standards' are to be maintained, and the supposed 'worst' schools raised to a level with the best, there can be no let up in pressure from these various sources. At Wroxham, in contrast, the life force of whole-school development is *belief in something worth striving for*. As we saw in the conclusion to Chapter 5, nurturing the seven dispositions was linked to a deeper moral purpose: creating an environment where everybody's learning can flourish, free from the limiting effects of ability labels. Fullan (2003) refers to this belief in something worth fighting for as 'the moral imperative', stressing its key importance as a driving force in school development. In his study of the role of school leaders in bringing about whole-system change, he argues that building better schools depends upon teacher passion, purpose and capacity, 'And you cannot get teachers working (together) like this without leaders at all levels guiding and supporting the process' (p. 5).

At Wroxham, as we noted in the conclusion to the previous section, belief in something worth striving for helped developments to become self-sustaining. From what staff told us, we know that it gave them new hope and purpose, enabling them to put the experience of being 'in the bottom set' behind them; it created the desire, the energy, the passion, the sense of personal agency, creativity and optimism needed to take on new ventures, rise to new challenges and go the extra mile if need be, while (for the most part) feeling excited and fulfilled by their endeavours rather than exhausted and put upon.

Beyond the 'training' culture: fostering a particular kind of learning

A second distinctive feature of the approach to school development at Wroxham is the particular kind of professional learning being encouraged, the kind of professional learning made possible by the seven dispositions. The Wroxham team are learning to see into the 'why?' of things, learning how to root every decision in the moral imperative. They are shaping a pedagogy that is underpinned *not* by skills, techniques, ready-made lesson plans, but by not-for-sale values – which at Wroxham are the moral values of inclusion, social justice, and the overriding principle of human educability. These same values shape curriculum developments and assessment practices. As the team become better informed, through reading, seminars, dialogue, they become more likely to make wiser decisions. But they go further than 'evidence-based-practice'; they evaluate the evidence against their principles. Every decision is congruent with their overall purpose, their vision of the equitable, harmonious learning without limits school.

This is the antithesis of the 'training' model of learning that has come to dominate professional development activity in recent years. The training model sidesteps thinking, questioning and inventiveness in favour of 'right' answers, 'what works' and 'best practice'. Pre-digested ideas about 'best practice' are 'delivered' to staff for them to implement in their classrooms. Training is often accompanied by voluminous packs of material, with key messages summarized on PowerPoint presentations. Prescriptiveness is so all-pervasive that, in some cases, even the training leaders have scripts to follow. The implicit message in the delivery style and in many packs of teaching materials, guidance, and in-service training boxes that have been sent into schools from official government agencies is that research has already reliably established 'what works'. The task for teachers therefore is essentially one of compliance, bringing their practice into closer alignment with what is recommended centrally, making progress towards the standard of perfection that 'best practice' represents. Teachers are expected to take research findings and their implications on trust, rather than engaging critically with the actual research, working out for themselves the relevance and applicability of the ideas to the children in their own classrooms, and considering how they fit with their most deeply held values and principles.

Compliance with externally derived, 'best practice' models is also promoted through the detailed, downloadable lesson plans covering most curriculum areas that have been made available to teachers in primary schools in an ill-advised attempt to foster improvements in teaching without adding to the burden of already over-pressed teachers. Noting the conscientious but vain efforts of one teacher to prepare an effective mathematics lesson using these plans, Bibby (2011: 110) points out that 'the burden being lifted is the need to think. And it is precisely the need to think that cannot be lifted.' Fear of the consequences of *not* following official guidance, even when non-statutory, has lent strength to this culture of compliance, often against teachers' own best judgement. It is not uncommon for experienced teachers on courses to be heard to enquire, in all due seriousness, if certain practices – or interpretations of the use of given materials – are 'allowed'.

At Wroxham, as we have seen, learning is open-ended. The teaching staff are no strangers to 'the need to think'. Wroxham teachers do take account of research and 'best practice' guidelines, as we have seen, but they do so as active, autonomous thinkers and learners. They engage with the ideas of others as part of a creative, learning process. Ideas are not taken on board ready-made, but feed into their understanding of how classroom conditions impact on learning capacity and what can be done to enrich and enhance learning opportunities. Leadership strategies respect and promote autonomous judgement; they are directed towards enabling staff to do their own learning, individually and collectively. There are no 'right ways', recommended best practices, or downloadable lesson plans, no invitation or excuse to side-step thinking. Instead there are generous resources, from within and beyond the collective, to nourish and inform reflection, as people work to develop their understandings and practices, exploring and expanding possibilities for practice, stimulated by an unwavering focus on children's learning.

Power and leadership: partnership and collaboration

This different view of professional learning has important consequences for teachers' sense of their own power and agency and for the distinctive nature of relationships between school leaders and their teaching teams. The training-delivery model assumes a hierarchy of power; ideas and dictats emanating from centralized agencies are passed down to school managers, frequently via local authorities, and from there disseminated to staff groups in schools by teachers with leadership responsibilities. This hierarchical approach reduces teachers' role to that of operative of other people's ideas. It is demeaning of teachers' expertise and also disempowering. The assumption is that 'what works' *will* work. But what if it does not? If teachers have been encouraged simply to apply ideas drawn from elsewhere, they do not have full control and ownership of the ideas needed to review and revise their practices and find new ways forward. Even more worryingly, if children do not learn when exposed to 'quality first teaching', then it seems logical to assume that the problem must lie with the child; there is no impetus or obligation for teachers to examine and develop their own practice. Hence the proliferation of booster groups and individualized support packages that have been introduced in recent years (e.g. DfES 2003b). At Wroxham, as we have shown, the approach to development ensures that teachers stay in control of their own learning. Their awareness of their own power, through the focus on children's learning and the cultivation of the seven dispositions, leads teachers to respond to difficulties by seeking to deepen their understanding of what is going on, working out for themselves what scope there is within current practices to lift limits and enhance learning opportunities.

As headteacher, Alison is strongly aware that teachers' sense of their own agency and power to change things for the better implies the need for a different kind of relationship between herself and her staff. This is why she was determined to dismantle hierarchies and position herself alongside her colleagues to share in the process of learning with them. She contrasts her own approach with the best practice model of leadership promoted through the training programme for the National Professional Qualification for Headteachers (NPQH), and generally commented upon favourably by Ofsted. What is expected of headteachers, she suggests, is to have their own strong vision and to implement it through staff meetings, staff training, lesson observations (with feedback and grades), performance management (with targets), data analysis to identify levels of progress, and use all these measurements to devise strategies for the school development plan. Alison, who is NPQH trained, started out accepting that she needed to try to follow this brief, but quickly began to realize that if she were to do all these things, they would not just absorb her time but have major implications for the kinds of relationships that she was able to build with staff. 'What's important is the *underpinning*

– how we engage with each other and enable each other's learning,' she said. As we have seen, even though Alison believes passionately in her own vision of the kind of school she wants to create, she sees no virtue in imposing her vision on others. Her approach from the outset was to communicate with people that they were invited to work with her in a genuine collaborative partnership, where ideas and insights would flow both ways. In working together, everyone had both power and responsibility. The development of The Wroxham School was something that they would all work on and achieve together.

Monitoring and accountability: intrinsic criteria, shared responsibility

The fourth area in which Wroxham's approach is distinctively different is with respect to systems of monitoring and accountability. At Wroxham, accountability is not primarily about *attainment*. Although the school is, of course, subject to the same external measures for monitoring school performance as every other maintained school in England (comparisons between actual and predicted attainment, comparisons between actual attainment and targets set for particular curriculum areas), these are not the measures used internally for the purpose of evaluation and monitoring. Accountability is intrinsically bound up with teachers' own intentions as they write their own plans, devise their own resources, introduce their own topics and projects and then monitor rigorously how the children are responding. When the teaching teams decide to make changes in their classroom practices, with a view to enhancing learning capacity, they do not just 'hope for the best' and assume that these changes will help the children to become more powerful, committed, enthusiastic learners. On the contrary, they follow up their decisions carefully and consistently, looking for signs that they are being successful, reflecting on what to do next to refine or improve their practice. If we look back at Chapters 3 and 4, we find many examples of teachers referring to the evidence they used to evaluate their decision making: for example, noting children's increased interest and investment in classroom activities, more 'spark', increases in confidence and control, more positive attitudes, an enhanced capacity to work together. It was because they saw these changes happening, saw for themselves children becoming better learners, that they were spurred on to extend freedom to learn into more areas of classroom experience.

The first *Learning without Limits* study drew attention to the potential for using questions based on teachers' purposes in teaching for transformability as a framework for wider accountability. The list of questions shown in Figure 6.4 could provide criteria for monitoring and evaluation intrinsic to teachers' own review and reflection processes. At Wroxham, once purposes became progressively shared, it became possible to embed systems for monitoring and accountability into the school-wide culture of learning, and so use the resources of the

Building confidence and emotional security	Do all the children feel emotionally safe, comfortable and positive about their participation in learning activities?
Strengthening feelings of competence and control	Do their classroom experiences strengthen or restore all children's feelings of competence and control?
Increasing enjoyment and purposefulness	Are classroom activities experienced by all children as interesting, enjoyable and purposeful?
Enhancing children's identities as learners	Do all the children experience sustained success and achievement in their learning, and recognition of that achievement?
Increasing hope and confidence in the future	Do all children recognize their own power to make a difference to their own future development? Do they develop constantly expanding conceptions of what is possible? Are they hopeful and confident for the future?
Increasing children's sense of acceptance and belonging	Do all children feel that they are looked upon by others as an equal member of the classroom community? Do they feel that their contributions are recognized and valued by their peers, as well as by their teacher?
Increasing children's capacity to work as a learning community	Have all children developed the skills needed to work together constructively as a team? Do they accept responsibility for working effectively as a learning community?
Providing successful access by all children to whatever knowledge, understanding and skills are intended to be the focus of a lesson	Have all children understood and engaged with the content and learning intentions of the lesson? Have they engaged in worthwhile learning in relation to these intentions?
Increasing relevance, enhancing meaning	Have all children found the content and tasks of the lesson relevant to their lives and concerns? Has it created intellectual connections for them? Has it opened up new horizons and led to recognition of new meanings and relevances?
Enhancing thinking, reasoning, explaining	Have all the children been helped to think, to talk about their thinking, to reflect on their learning and what helps them to learn?

Figure 6.4   Using questions as a starting point for monitoring and accountability

Source: Adapted from Hart *et al.* (2004).

collective to support and enhance the review, reflection and learning undertaken by each teacher individually. In Chapter 2, we described the work of the faculty teams, which replaced subject leadership by individuals. The teams, which have continued to flourish and develop since that time, assume shared responsibility for the quality of experiences and opportunities offered to children in their curriculum areas. They also take on the task of monitoring the quality of children's learning in each area. Included in the many activities undertaken by the faculty teams is sharing and discussing samples of children's work, not in order to agree on 'levels' but to deepen understanding of children's learning in all its rich variety, to recognize and describe progress in ways that do not reduce its complexity to crude numerical values, and to share thoughts and insights into how it might be enhanced. As we have also noted, Alison does not need, or want, to do observations purely for performance management purposes. Instead she assures quality in teaching through her many learning conversations with colleagues, in and out of the classroom.

To summarize, then, we have identified four distinctive features of the approach to school development evolving at Wroxham (see Table 6.3).

Table 6.3 Four distinctive features of school development at Wroxham

Feature	Standards agenda Perfectibility approach	Alternative approach Transformability approach
Impetus for improvement	Extrinsic Externally imposed pressure	Intrinsic Passion, striving for something you believe in
Professional development	Training model Disseminate known 'best practice', downloaded teaching plans, 'what works'	Create conditions for professional learning to flourish Strengthen dispositions of autonomous professional learners
Power and leadership	Top-down initiatives Invested in senior leadership team Value placed on teacher compliance	Partnership Head as lead learner Collaboration Value placed on teacher power, autonomy and creative, collective endeavour
Monitoring and accountability	Extrinsic criteria based on attainments Comparison with local and national norms, targets Performance management Observation and grading	Intrinsic criteria based on teachers' purposes Embedded in structures and processes to support professional learning Shared responsibility Collaborative learning

These distinctive features find many parallels with the independent findings of the *Cambridge Primary Review* (Alexander, 2010), the most comprehensive study of English primary education since the Plowden Report (CACE 1967). The Review stresses the need to link developments in primary schools firmly to the pursuit of fundamental principles: 'equity and empathy, entitlement, engagement, empowerment, expertise and excellence' (p. 4). It makes similar criticisms of the view of teaching and professional learning reflected in the approach to pedagogy of the national agencies, which reduces teaching 'to tips which can be lifted ready-made from "best practice" websites without regard for the context of their application' (p. 7). What is needed instead, the Review argues, is an alternative view of professionalism [in which] 'in relation to anything he or she does, a teacher is able to give a coherent justification citing (i) evidence, (ii) pedagogical principle, and (iii) educational aim' (p. 308). The Review also notes the importance of re-empowering leaders and teachers who have been subject to centralist control and a regime of high-stakes testing and accountability:

> The focus needs to be one which enables school leaders to develop a culture in which internal school accountability for the quality of teaching and learning precedes and shapes external accountability. This rests on the development of trust and openness to collegial support and challenge.
>
> (Alexander 2010: 507)

While The Wroxham School is subject to the same expectations of year-on-year improvements in attainment as other schools, this awareness of how the school will be judged externally does not drive or distort development. When people are talking about learning with each other or with the children, they do not usually focus directly on levels and what can be done to boost them. They trust that better attainment will come about as the by-product of all that they are doing to enhance conditions for learning and enable children to become better learners. They trust that the impact on children's learning will not only be noticeable in terms of their own criteria – the rich, open view of learning and learners that they are seeking to foster – but also in the criteria by which their work is judged by others, namely in their measured attainments across National Curriculum levels. As we have seen, their trust has been amply rewarded by rapid improvements in children's measured attainment. In 2006, Wroxham was one of the top performing schools in terms of contextual value-added scores. In the most recent inspection, Wroxham was awarded the grade of 'outstanding' in all categories, showing that it *is* possible for schools to diverge from the official path, yet for this to be welcomed and evaluated highly by Ofsted.

Relevance, applicability and implications

We now turn to the question of what others can learn from the experience of the Wroxham staff working together to create learning without limits. Undoubtedly there are many people who share similar values and who would like to develop an approach to school improvement that is in harmony with and actively promotes their values rather than working against them. But are there lessons of general applicability, for school leaders, policy makers and practitioners, that can be drawn out from this study of a single school at a particular point in time?

Many of the details of our story of Wroxham would, of course, have been different if the research had been carried out a few years later, when developments building on the foundations described in Chapter 2 would have had more time to take shape and expand. As we noted in the conclusion to that chapter, school improvement inspired by the core ideas of *Learning without Limits* has no final end point. Since the data collection phase of the research, the Wroxham staff have been continuing to develop their thinking and practice. Martyn, whose interest in outdoor education was just becoming established when he organized the Robin Hood Day, discussed in Chapter 3, is now a qualified forest school leader. His article 'Come rain or shine: a whole school approach to Forest School' (Vandewalle 2010) draws on his experience of leading the school's recently developed programme of outdoor education. Jo, now teaching Year 6, has continued to develop the self-assessment journals discussed in Chapter 3, which gradually took on broader uses as learning journals and later became online blogs. She is also a mentor working across the new Teaching School alliance set up by Wroxham in September 2011. Sophie, whose approach to working with her challenging class was described in Chapter 4, is now drawing on her experience of being effectively supported by her school-based mentor to develop her own approaches to working with colleagues in her role as a leading mathematics teacher. Cheryl, who noticed how children's attitudes to learning and relationships flourished when she ceased to use ability grouping and offered more choices in her classroom, now has responsibility for inclusive practice and family support at Wroxham and across the alliance. Alison now combines the headship of Wroxham with leading a national network for the Cambridge Primary Review. She continues to publish in a variety of journals; in a recent paper, 'Beyond assessment levels', she describes the alternative assessment practices currently being developed at Wroxham (Peacock 2011).

There have also been some changes in staffing. Simon has become a headteacher in a neighbouring borough; he is drawing on his experience at Wroxham to lead the staff of his new school along similar lines. Darrelle has retired but keeps in close contact with the school. New teachers have joined the school, bringing fresh knowledge, experience and perspectives to enrich the work of the whole team. However, while many changes have occurred and new developments taken place, the fundamental principles and commitment to ongoing professional learning of the particular kind we have described remain unchanged. We are confident that the insights that have emerged through the study do have enduring relevance and applicability to people in other contexts – for school staffs craving for better, more powerful and humane ways of approaching school improvement; for individual teachers wondering how best to use their power to foster children's learning; for school leaders who find their values increasingly compromised by the pressures of the standards agenda; for teacher educators working in institutions of higher education who are finding their efforts to sustain powerful models of professional learning on their courses becoming increasingly constrained. We are hopeful, too, if not naively optimistic, that the experience of Wroxham will provide an object lesson for policy makers, showing that another way *is* possible for school improvement and why this way is better: better because it is self-sustaining and constantly self-renewing, leading to better attainment by making the experience of learning more engaging, worthwhile and life-enhancing for everybody. In the following pages, we consider what lessons might be drawn by these various groups, beginning with some of the implications for individual teachers.

Implications for individual teachers

Although our study was designed to explore the scope that exists beyond individual teachers' practice for enhancing children's learning capacity, we believe that there are some messages for individual teachers, whatever the contexts in which they are working, that can be drawn from our study of Wroxham School. A first message is an important point of clarification for everyone interested in the developments taking place in the school: that the story of Wroxham is not about abandoning ability grouping, and it is not about mixed-ability teaching. It is about a deeper and much more far-reaching project: rejecting fixed ability thinking, in all its guises, and with all its negative effects on children, teachers, curriculum and assessment. It is about replacing the fatalism of ability labels with a more hopeful, powerful and empowering view of learners and learning.

The development work, described in Chapters 3 and 4, is a detailed practical illustration of what one group of teachers did to transform their children's learning capacity. We hope it will be a source of inspiration and guidance to other teachers wanting to develop their practices based on a similar commitment to the essential educability of all children. But their example offers no recipe or blueprint for other teachers. Perhaps the most important message other teachers can draw from the Wroxham experience is that there is no one way, and certainly no *right* way to develop practices free from ideas of fixed ability. As we showed in Chapter 3, all the Wroxham teachers worked differently. They each thought things out for themselves and made their own choices in the name of transformability. Although we found a strong measure of agreement between them about elements of pedagogy, this does not mean that either these broad elements of pedagogy or the strategies and practices to which they gave rise are transferable to other contexts. Extending freedom to learn is the Wroxham teachers' shared interpretation of what they can do to enable children to become more powerful, enthusiastic learners. It illustrates just one approach to enhancing learning capacity, as understood by these teachers. But there is no short cut; all teachers have to do their own thinking and arrive at their own understandings in order to make transforming choices for the children in their classrooms. It is the thinking – not just the practices that result – that enables teachers to transform learning capacity. The teachers' purposes, the principles (co-agency, everybody and trust), and the conviction that teachers can transform children's learning capacity are all directly transferable. What results from their application in new contexts will depend on many things: the context, the children, the teacher's knowledge, understanding and experience; it will depend, too, on what emerges as a result of examining the interplay between classroom conditions and learners' states of mind in that situation, at that particular point in time. As Sophie discovered, strategies that have proved to be enabling with one group of children may need to be rethought and renegotiated with the next class.

While it is true that there is no one right way, however, there is a strong measure of agreement, among the Wroxham staff, about what *not* to do. To appreciate more fully how the principles inform teachers' decision making, we need to look at what they are not thinking and doing, as well as at what they are thinking and doing. People at Wroxham do not assume that differences in attainment can be explained by the limited potential of some children. They do not sort pupils into ability groups and differentiate their teaching on the basis of predicting what each group will achieve. They do not see a child's struggle with a particular concept as evidence of a lack of ability, but as evidence that this is an important site of learning for the child and for themselves, challenging them to review their own practices and seek ways to enhance learning opportunities.

Linked to this set of practices is the finding that Wroxham teachers increasingly avoided the language of 'special educational needs' to talk about children. Just as ability labels had become increasingly redundant, so too had ways of thinking, talking about and responding to *some* children that set them apart from the rest of the class. Though there are children with statements in the school and children whose learning staff are concerned about, nevertheless these children are not perceived by their teachers or by other children as a distinct group and are not singled out. Teaching staff respond to difficulties experienced by these children, as they do for *all* children, by noticing and questioning what happens in the classroom, by analysing how the children respond to opportunities to learn, and working out what they themselves can do to create more enabling conditions for learning. Finding ways forward is treated as a shared responsibility, pooling ideas and drawing on collective memory, so that no member of staff is left to struggle on their own. Wherever possible, people look for inclusive ways of responding to individual difficulties, through developments in their practice intended to enhance everybody's learning.

A practical starting point, for an individual teacher committed to the learning without limits ideal, might be to take the set of questions in Figure 6.4 and reflect on classroom experience through the lens of one or more of the questions; to ask, for example, do classroom experiences strengthen all learners' feelings of competence and control? If not, what might be getting in the way? Then, using the principles of co-agency, trust and everybody, teachers might consider what more they could do to strengthen those feelings of confidence and control. Having decided on something practical to try that is congruent with the three principles, then they might watch carefully for signs that indicate children are feeling more competent and in control, reflect on what has happened and make adjustments accordingly. While this might look like the sort of reflection that all good teachers do, what distinguishes teachers committed to learning without limits is that they start out from the assumption that change *is* possible, and for *all* children. Competence and control are not fixed, stable states, greater or lesser according to people's innate ability. Rather, everybody can and should experience feelings of competence and control, and their learning will be inhibited if they do not. Everybody's learning capacity can be increased if teachers use their power and insight to find ways to increase feelings of competence and control.

The framework of dispositions may also provide a useful reflective tool for teachers who recognize these ways of being and learning as characteristic of the kind of teacher that they themselves are committed to being and becoming in their own professional work. We hope that the Wroxham story provides encouragement for other teachers to take pride in their capacity to focus intently on learning, to notice and question what happens in the classroom, to analyse how children respond to opportunities to learn, and to use their power to take action to transform learning capacity. When they are confronting a challenging situation, for example a distressed parent or child whose learning is not flourishing, the dispositions, as well as the principles, may provide useful guidance for teachers to help them approach the challenge, for example, with openness, empathy and inventiveness, thus affirming their sense of personal identity, while fostering their professional learning.

A further message that can be drawn from the Wroxham experience is the importance, for individual teachers, of nourishing their own learning through contact with the ideas of others, and through engaging critically with literature and research that offers new insights into what limits learning and what can be done to expand and enhance learning opportunities. Specialist subject knowledge as well as generalist literature on curriculum, pedagogy and assessment can be an important source of new insights. For example, mathematician Boaler, whose research was referred to in Chapters 3 and 5, provides a powerful illustration of how children's capacity to learn mathematics is related to the kind of mathematics that is taught in schools. Many children have difficulty with mathematics, she contends, because 'a very narrow subject is taught to children, that is nothing like the maths of the world or the maths that mathematicians use'. Drawing on her own research, she argues that when 'real mathematics' is taught, involving 'problem solving, creating ideas and representations, exploring puzzles, discussing methods and many different ways of working' (Boaler 2009: 2), then children become better and more successful learners of mathematics. Teachers committed to transforming learning capacity will be constantly on the lookout for such resources to enrich their understanding of the interplay between the external and internal forces that affect children's capacity to learn and open up new avenues in their search for new possibilities for practice.

Finally, recognition of the power of the collective, in the Wroxham story, carries a message for individual teachers to find like-minded people to work with, within and beyond their schools. We urge teachers, wherever possible, to do their thinking in the company of others, seeking help, sharing complexities, supporting each other by building collective power in schools, local networks and contacts with higher education institutions.

Implications for school leaders

Many school leaders and staff subscribe to the same values as the Wroxham team but have, understandably, found it risky and challenging to resist pressure to follow approaches to school development that comply with the officially sponsored model and its associated expectations for good practice described above. The Wroxham story, therefore, is one of hope. It shows that there *is* another way, that an alternative, principled and practicable approach to school development is possible. Earlier in this chapter, we explored in detail the distinctive features of this alternative approach. We hope this will be useful to school leaders in recognizing how the essential tasks required of them to ensure quality and accountability can be accomplished in ways that are in harmony with and actively promote their values base, rather than working against them.

The Wroxham story provides a detailed analysis of the role of leadership in developing a school inspired by *Learning without Limits* ideas and principles, which we hope will be of interest and use to leaders in other schools. One important message is about the importance of giving absolute priority to creating conditions that will enable professional learning to flourish. This includes creating a stable environment to enable everybody to focus their energies on learning. Moreover, it is not just *any* sort of learning that is being fostered, as we discussed earlier on in this chapter, but the kind of professional learning reflected in and made possible by the dispositions described in Chapter 5. We have shown that the pedagogical principles (co-agency, everybody, trust) do also apply to leaders' decision making when deciding on strategies to support adult learning and have illustrated the kinds of strategies to which they led when applied to the task of building a powerful team of professional learners. We believe that these principles, the dispositions and their part in creating conditions for transformability (in so far as we understand them at present, for adults and children) are transferable to other schools; the strategies to which they have given rise at Wroxham, in this particular context, at this time, by these people, will change over time (as we have seen above in the developments at Wroxham since the research period) and are not directly transferable. Though the Wroxham story provides an illustration, school leaders will need to do their own analysis and generate their own repertoire of strategies, from their specific knowledge and experiences of their own particular contexts, in relation to their own colleagues.

The Wroxham story also provides a stimulus for other leaders to reflect on the kind of relationships needed to foster these sorts of developments. How are these relationships affected by practices associated with the standards agenda model of improvement, for example the demeaning practice of labelling teachers as 'weak', 'satisfactory' and 'good'. Subjecting teachers to such judgements is not just damaging psychologically; the labels profoundly undermine the relationships of co-agency that, as the Wroxham story shows, lie at the very heart of the alternative approach to school improvement described in this book. At Wroxham, there was and is no ability labelling of children or staff; the desire and need to learn is shared by everybody, and indeed is recognized as a mark of expertise, a matter of professional pride within the teaching team. This is a wonderful example of the principle of 'everybody' in action. At Wroxham, everybody learns. 'Everybody' of course includes the headteacher who embodies the dispositions in her daily dealings with staff, parents and children; in her relationships with them she takes on the role of partner in learning; she is also deeply committed to nourishing her own learning and forging connections to support her own thinking and development, in order to enrich the support she is able to offer the teaching team.

Furthermore, there is a message for school leaders about harnessing the power of the collective. The power of the headteacher to move the school in the direction of her vision was and is conditional on the extent to which she can make all parties feel that they are working towards something worth striving for, that their contribution counts, and the extent to which everybody in the school community therefore uses their powers to support these developments. The Wroxham team show us that it is possible to do school development differently, working with the grain of teachers' thinking, rather than imposing things onto them; they demonstrate that a school inspired by the *Learning without*

Limits vision can be recognized as outstanding by Ofsted, achieve creditable test results, and be warmly appreciated by both parents and children. As one parent shrewdly observed: 'I don't want [Michael] to feel that there are limits. I don't want him to believe that way. I want him to think broader – anything and everything is possible – I think that's what he's going to get here.'

Finally, and perhaps most importantly, there is a need to join forces, to share ideas, experiences and purposes with other schools and other educationists who are working to develop principled approaches to school improvement. In exploring the ways in which the approach to school development at Wroxham differs from the approach sponsored by the standards agenda, we are not suggesting that this is the *only* alternative approach currently being developed. We know, for example, that there are many schools, in the UK and in many countries throughout the world, that continue to use the rich resource provided by the *Index for Inclusion* (Booth *et al.* 2000; Booth and Ainscow 2002, 2011) to support their development work. Using the *Index,* the authors argue, 'is not an additional initiative but a way of improving schools according to inclusive values' (Booth and Ainscow 2011: 19). Inclusion is 'a commitment to particular values that account for a wish to overcome exclusion and promote participation' (Booth and Ainscow 2011: 21). Booth (2011) argues that:

> Those engaged in the principled development of education may form a far larger group than is sometimes recognised. People conceive of their development efforts as falling under a variety of labels such as comprehensive community education, democratic education, anti-bias/anti-discrimination education, equalities education, healthy schools, sustainability education, global citizenship, values and rights based education, critical pedagogy, learning without ability labelling and non-violent education.
>
> (Booth 2011: 46)

What is needed, Booth suggests, is a superordinate concept, such as 'inclusion', to unite all these approaches by creating common ground at the level of values upon which alliances can be made.

Implications for teacher education providers

Our study of Wroxham has shown that creating learning without limits is dependent on powerful professional learning of a particular kind. What does this mean for teacher educators committed to *Learning without Limits* principles and values for the kind of courses available? There is an important partnership role for higher education institutions to play in continuing to support and foster professional learning of this kind. Teacher educators (in England) have found themselves increasingly constrained by government specification of what students must cover, and how much time must be spent on particular curriculum areas. There is also increasing pressure on funding, both direct to schools and also in Higher Education Institutions, to support teachers' continuing professional learning. Nevertheless, in view of the fact that the Wroxham team, subject to similar external pressures, did find a way of living by principle, we hope that our research offers renewed inspiration to teacher education providers to review the kind of provision available, to maintain a sense of the values and principles that matter, to resist pressure to deliver training programmes, instead of developing courses that foster autonomous professional learning.

The dispositions provide a possible framework for review and reflection, which might support teacher education providers in reconsidering their provision, in articulating for themselves the dispositions that they aim to foster (if not these, others), and in considering how the choices they make relating to course curricula and activities reflect the core principles of co-agency, everybody and trust. We hope that our study will support the design of courses that foster the dispositions of the powerful educator. Such courses would give teachers opportunities to examine and think through carefully selected examples of important alternatives, drawn from contemporary and classic educational thinkers and researchers, who have contributed to the accumulating inheritance of the teaching profession. These courses would also encourage teachers to draw guidance and inspiration from each other, building knowledge, strength and courage to make transforming choices for all children. We are greatly encouraged to learn that the core ideas and principles arising from the first *Learning without Limits* study have already been embedded in courses of initial teacher education. At the University of Aberdeen, student teachers following an elective course on *Learning without Limits* use these ideas and principles as a framework for reflection while on school placement (Florian and Linklater 2010). At the University of Hertfordshire the staff team responsible for programmes of initial teacher education drew on *Learning without Limits* ideas to eradicate the use of fixed-ability language (high/middle/low abilities) in school placement documentation as one way of addressing their concern that students were thinking about and labelling children in terms of fixed ability. More information on both these initiatives can be found at http://www.learningwithoutlimits.co.uk/

Implications for policy makers

We are now several steps closer than at the end of the original study to showing both that an alternative approach to school improvement is possible and also what it looks like in practice at one school. We have shown that there is a better and more humane way of encouraging schools to grow and flourish, free from the deprofessionalizing experience of external threat, constant surveillance and top-down pressure to implement externally generated solutions to perceived problems, which are divorced from the specificity of particular schools, communities and groups of children. The Wroxham example shows that a school committed to learning without limits is, almost by definition, a school that is learning, developing, improving. Policy makers can trust in the expertise of school leaders committed to these core ideas and principles to create the conditions for professional learning to flourish, drawing on the commitment of teachers to enhancing children's life chances, their expertise and their fascination with learning. Policy makers can trust in the professionalism of teachers, given supportive conditions, to use their power to transform learning capacity, to keep thinking, to keep trying, to keep looking for ways to unlock learning.

We are aware that, when this book appears in print, there may have been changes in national policy that will present new challenges. As we write, a major review of the National Curriculum is under way and it is suggested that the practice of using levels to plan and report on learning may be abandoned. Indeed, a recently published report by the expert panel charged with advising this review (DfE 2011) maps out key dimensions of an alternative way of 'judging progression' (p. 44), to replace rigid stratification of learning by levels, citing *Learning without Limits* approaches as evidence that 'this kind of approach is both practically feasible and educationally justified' (p. 49). But this welcome commendation does not make our critique redundant nor does it make any less necessary our search for better ways for schools to carry out their responsibilities. The members of the expert panel clearly share our concerns about the limits placed on learning by ideas of fixed ability (p. 45) and recommend basing future policy on the assumption that all children have the 'capability for improvement' (p. 48). In our view, the challenge will be to ensure that, if levels are dismantled, the space created by their absence is not filled by a resurgence of ability labelling and ability-based practices. New views of intelligence provide strong corroboration for our rejection of fixed ability thinking (see Appendix C). They provide an important resource for teachers to help resist pressures to label and categorize young people. However, they do not in themselves offer an adequate alternative view of learning capacity upon which policy might be developed. What is needed, as argued in *Learning without Limits*, is a concept of learning capacity that reflects the complex interplay of factors – between what is going on in children's minds and the conditions made available to them for learning in school – that affect children's capacity to learn in any given situation. School development needs to be organized, as at Wroxham, to enable everybody's energies to be focused on understanding how school experience impacts on learning capacity and using that understanding to take actions that will progressively enable *all* children to become more committed, powerful, enthusiastic learners. Only if policy supports such a focus will we be able to capitalize on the enormous scope for enhancing children's learning capacity that exists in our schools, and enable improvement to become self-sustaining.

The future in the making: where do we go from here?

As our story of Wroxham draws to a close, we realize that there is nevertheless much still to learn. We hope that others, during their journeys, will seek out mutual support and maybe take up some of the issues we identify here as ripe for further exploration. One such area is the involvement of parents in genuine partnership with schools, and tapping into learning at home as a resource for staff learning and curriculum development. We recognize that, in both this and our first study, understanding of how learning capacity can be increased has been focused on *within*-school influences. We need to develop a fuller appreciation of how influences *beyond* the school are also brought into the analysis, not in order to acknowledge what is beyond the scope of teachers' action, but to offer empowering new insight into what can be done within the school to enable children's learning to flourish. Although in our account of developments at Wroxham we have not addressed issues of ethnicity, class, gender and disability explicitly, it is our conviction that the analysis of inter-acting influences that lies at the heart of teachers' power to make a difference means that these issues can be taken into account in an equitable and empow-ering way, when the principle of transformability inspires approaches to school improvement. There is a strong heritage of ideas in this area to draw on in formulating ways forward for research and practice, as the following three examples show.

A seminal study by Tizard and Hughes (1984) drew attention to striking differences between the language used by pre-school, working class girls at home and at school. Without the input of parents, teachers had no way of discovering these differences for themselves, so they took the evidence of limited language use at school as a fair representation of children's actual linguistic capabilities. Since no such differences between home and school were found with the middle class children, Tizard and Hughes argued that something about the differences between the linguistic patterns of exchange at home and in the nursery school was inhibiting the working class children from using language to express themselves fully. Analysing these patterns of language opened up important insights into shifts that might be made in adult–child interactions in the school setting to enable children to use and develop their linguistic resources more fully, as they did in their lively sustained conversations at home.

Another important source of related ideas is the work of Gregory (Gregory 1994, 1998, 2000; Gregory *et al.* 1996) who, since the 1990s, has carried out a number of studies exploring how differences in cultural practices between the home and the school – for example relating to the acquisition of literacy – can cause children to lose faith in what they are being taught at school and become disaffected. In one memorable article Gregory (1993) explored in detail how this occurred to a young Chinese boy within one year of entering school as an enthusiastic, energetic learner. Gregory's work shows why understanding these beyond-school influences is so important, how it can help teachers to understand the genesis of limits on learning, and allow teachers to focus their efforts more accurately in finding ways to prevent or overcome them.

Moreover, in a study of children's learning at home, Maddock (2006) shows the richness and variety of learning happening in the homes of children who are judged by their teachers to be lower attainers and whose parents are not visibly supportive of the school's work. She shows how, in the home and outside world, the children engaged in a rich programme of learning activities and demonstrated knowledge, skills and resourcefulness that did not appear in their behaviour at school. The study raises many important questions worth further investigation about why this should be, what was happening in the transition between home and school and what might therefore be done *within* the school context to enable such children to learn with the same verve, creativity and competence as in their out-of-school activities. Partnership with parents must be a crucial component of any strategy, since it is only through the testimony of parents and children that teachers can find out about the interests and competences of children that may not be revealed in school settings.

One way of exploring in more detail how beyond-school influences can help to empower teaching staff to take action to increase children's capacity to learn within school might be to carry out case studies of individual children's progress over a relatively extended period of time. Building on previous research on innovative thinking and values-based assessment (Hart 2000; Drummond 2012), and case studies like those carried out by Armstrong (2006), could help to illuminate what goes on in the processes of observation, interpretation, analysis and judgement that inform teachers' thinking and decision making with respect to individual children; they could explore how a range of cultural influences impact on teachers' understanding and children's engagement with learning activities; they would provide a more finely grained understanding of how teachers' choices and actions affect the learning of individual children, and how this understanding leads to further enquiry and action. They would also trace how thinking about individuals can stimulate questioning and inspire generalized ideas about what might be done to enhance conditions for learning for the whole class.

A second important area for further research is the contribution that specialist subject knowledge can make to our understanding of the scope for enhancing learning capacity. One area where research is already taking place is mathematics. In this book, we have referred at a number of points to the important insights provided by Boaler, through her research in the

UK and USA. There is also the seminal work of Watson (Watson 2001, 2006, 2011; Watson and De Geest 2008; Watson *et al.* 2003), who has for many years been exploring ways of raising the attainment and enhancing the mathematical thinking of lower attaining secondary students. Her work is based on the conviction that previously lower attaining students can be helped to become better learners of mathematics by being exposed to the challenging opportunities for learning mathematics usually reserved for those perceived as the most able mathematicians. Similar research or reviews of existing research and practice need to be undertaken in every curriculum area in order to tease out subject-specific insights into how limits on learning come into being and how to create conditions that will enable all children to become better learners of English, languages, science, geography, technology and so on.

Other writers and researchers are working on a broader perspective. For example, many of the themes that appear in our account of the school-wide culture of learning at Wroxham can also be found in *Radical Education and the Common School: A Democratic Alternative*, by Fielding and Moss (2011), a book threaded through with the authors' passionate commitment to 'the insistent, persistent affirmation of possibility' (p. 82). They argue for a 'fundamentally redesigned but pragmatically possible alternative for education and schooling' (p. 2). This radical possibility can and has been enacted in real-life schools: the authors introduce their vision with vignettes of the preschools of Reggio Emilia, Italy, and a secondary modern school in Stepney, a tough area in the East End of London, Saint-George-in-the-East, which became, under the headship of Alex Bloom in the years 1945–55, hugely well known among progressive educators worldwide. Fielding and Moss give other, more recent examples of schools that embody the characteristics that they see as necessary for truly radical democratic education, and convincingly conclude that 'these transformative alternatives' illustrate, even if only in small ongoing ways:

> . . . the grounded possibility of doing things significantly differently . . . When we actually encounter these radical alternatives, it is in large part their brute reality, their enacted denial of injustice and inhumanity and their capacity to live out a more fulfilling, generous view of human flourishing that in turn move us to think and act differently.
>
> (Fielding and Moss 2011: 163)

We ourselves have been reluctant to draw out implications from our study for teachers and leaders working in secondary schools. The massive difference of scale, the complexity of organization as well as the influence of adolescence and emerging adulthood, make it difficult to generalize from a study of a one-form entry primary school. The question if and how whole-school developments inspired by the principles of *Learning without Limits* can be fostered at secondary level remains an important and open area for further research. It may be that the place to begin, in secondary schools, to foster a sense of collective identity and purpose, a shared understanding of what can be done to enhance learning capacity, is at departmental level. Anne Watson, whose research in mathematics was referred to above, recently carried out a study of three schools who reconstructed their approaches to mathematics teaching to ensure that all students, regardless of prior attainment, were exposed to challenging mathematics. The study found that forms of support for teachers' learning, very similar to those provided at Wroxham, were needed in order to enable the teachers to develop their mathematical teaching practices and adjust their perceptions of what previously lower attainers might achieve. Readers who are interested in following up these developments at secondary level are urged to visit the project website (http://www.cmtp.co.uk).

There is also much to be considered in addressing issues within initial teacher education and continuing professional development. Research is already under way at the University of Aberdeen, to investigate the impact of the use of *Learning without Limits* core ideas and principles on the thinking and practice of student teachers both during and after their course (Florian and Linklater 2010). One of the original team of nine teachers who participated in the first study is now working at Bishop Grosseteste University College, Lincoln. She undertook a study of teaching assistants' experience of learning on a Foundation Degree course (Taylor 2009). The study led to new understanding of factors contributing to successful learning in HE, including the role of workplace experience, the learner's self theories and motivation, tutor beliefs regarding ability and the tutor's role. At the Faculty of Education in Cambridge, teachers have the opportunity to participate in a master's degree module based around *Learning without Limits* ideas. Course themes include identifying the effects of fixed-ability thinking on teachers, children and curriculum; exploring alternative ways of conceptualizing teaching, learning and school improvement; constructing a principled pedagogical approach to increasing the learning capacity of all learners; teachers and children working as co-agents in learning; pupil consultation and power sharing. These various courses offer rich opportunities for exploring how people new to the ideas engage with them, how they make them their own, if they do, and how they embody them in their developing practice. Readers interested to find out more about ongoing research and resources related to the *Learning without Limits* project are invited to visit our website (http://www.learningwithoutlimits.co.uk/).

Final thoughts

Education today needs fewer large-scale quantitative studies comparing performance on pre-determined outcomes and more

> critical case-studies of possibility, opportunities to enrich our imagi-
> nation and vocabulary.
>
> (Fielding and Moss 2011: 16)

Fielding and Moss make this challenging recommendation in the context of their argument that radical alternatives to 'today's educational mainstream' are both urgently needed and, more importantly, practically possible. We contend that this book is just such a critical case-study of possibility. In advocating an approach to school improvement inspired by *Learning without Limits* principles, we do not claim that changes can be made instantly or problems fixed once and for all. Development of this kind is deep-rooted and long-lasting; it entails fundamental changes in thinking, belief and ways of being. Our study shows that it is possible and does work. We hope that reading the story of Wroxham will be an enriching experience; we hope that our readers' imaginations will be stimulated by our account of how the staff of one school has found ways of transforming teaching and learning, curriculum and peda-gogy, reshaping their school, in Fielding and Moss's inspiring phrase, as 'a place to help realise human potentiality and a democratic way of life' (2011: 72) We hope too that our readers' vocabularies will be extended, as they come to understand how familiar structures and relationships can be given new meaning, when they are pressed into the service of the big ideas at the heart of this book. To believe in fixed ability is to believe in fixed futures and the limited power of teachers. To believe in the transformability of learning capacity is to embrace the convictions we expressed in the opening pages: that human development is not predictable, that children's futures are unknowable, that education has the power to enhance the lives of all.

References

Alexander, R. J. (1984) *Primary Teaching*. Eastbourne: Holt, Reinhart and Winston.

Alexander, R. J. (2001) *Culture and Pedagogy: International Comparisons in Primary Education*. Oxford: Blackwell.

Alexander, R. J. (2008) *Essays on Pedagogy*. London: Routledge.

Alexander, R. J. (ed.) (2010) *Children, Their World, Their Education. Final Report and Recommendations of the Cambridge Primary Review*. London: Routledge.

Armstrong, M. (2006) *Children Writing Stories*. Maidenhead: Open University Press.

Balchin, T., Hymer, B. and Matthews, D. J. (2009) *The Routledge International Companion to Gifted Education*. London: Routledge.

Ball, S. (1981) *Beachside Comprehensive: A Case-Study of Secondary Schooling*. Cambridge: Cambridge University Press.

Bath, C. (2009) *Learning to Belong. Exploring Young Children's Participation at the Start of School*. London: Routledge.

Bernstein, B. (1971) Education cannot compensate for society, in B. Cosin, R. Dale, G. Esland and D. Swift (eds) *School and Society: A Sociological Reader*. London: Routledge and Kegan Paul.

Bibby, T. (2011) *Education – An Impossible Profession? Psychoanalytic Explorations of Learning and Classrooms*. London: Routledge.

Black, P. J. and Wiliam, D. (1998) *Inside the Black Box: Raising Standards through the Curriulum*. London: Kings College School of Education.

Bloom, B. S. (1976) *Human Characteristics and School Learning*. New York London: McGraw-Hill.

Boaler, J. (1997a) Setting, social class and survival of the quickest, *British Educational Research Journal*, 23(5): 575–95.

Boaler, J. (1997b) When even the winners are losers: evaluating the experiences of 'top set' students, *Journal of Curriculum Studies*, 29(2): 165–82.

Boaler, J. (2005) The 'psychological prisons' from which they never escaped: the role of ability grouping in reproducing social class inequalities, *FORUM for Promoting 3–19 Comprehensive Education*, 47(2 & 3): 135–43.

Boaler, J. (2009). *The Elephant in the Classroom. Helping Children Learn and Love Maths*. London: Souvenir Press.

Boaler, J., Wiliam, D. and Brown, M. (2000) Students' experiences of ability grouping: disaffection, polarisation and the construction of failure, *British Educational Research Journal*, 26(5): 631–48.

Booth, T. (2011) Curricula for the common school: what shall we tell our children?, *FORUM for Promoting 3–19 Comprehensive Education*, 53(1): 31–47.

Booth, T. and Ainscow, M. (2002) *Index for Inclusion. Developing Learning and Participation in Schools*, revised ed. Bristol: Centre for Studies on Inclusive Education.

Booth, T. and Ainscow, M. (2011) *Index for Inclusion. Developing Learning and Participation in Schools*. Bristol: Centre for Studies on Inclusive Education.

Booth, T., Ainscow, M., Black-Hawkins, K., Vaughan, M. and Shaw, L. (2000) *Index for Inclusion. Developing Learning and Participation in Schools*. Bristol: Centre for Studies on Inclusive Education in collaboration with Centre for Educational Needs, Manchester and Centre for Educational Research, Canterbury Christ Church University College.

Bourdieu, P. (1976) The school as a conservative force: scholastic and cultural inequalities, in R. Dale, G. Esland and M. MacDonald (eds) *Schooling and Capitalism*. London: Routledge and Kegan Paul.

Brice Heath, S. (1983) *Ways with Words: Language, Life and Work in Communities and Classrooms*. Cambridge: Cambridge University Press.

Bruner, J. (1996) *The Culture of Education*. Cambridge, MA: Harvard University Press.

CACE (Central Advisory Council for Education) (1967) *Children and Their Primary Schools (Plowden Report)*. London: HMSO.

Chitty, C. (2009) *Eugenics, Race, Intelligence and Education*. London: Continuum.

Clark, L. (2010) Privately-educated Michael Gove says 'rich, thick kids' do better than 'poor, clever children', *Mail Online*. Accessed 30 June 2011 from http://www.dailymail.co.uk/news/article-1298425/.

Claxton, G. (1990) *Teaching to Learn. A Direction for Education*. London: Cassell.

Coard, B. (1971) *How the West Indian Child Is Made Educationally Subnormal in the British School System: The Scandal of the Black Child in Schools in Britain*. London: New Carribean Workers Association.

Croll, P. and Moses, D. (1985) *One in Five: The Assessment and Incidence of Special Education Needs*. London: Routledge and Kegan Paul.

Cuffaro, H. K. (1995) *Experimenting with the World: John Dewey and the Early Childhood Classroom*. New York London: Teachers College Press.

de Bono, E. (2000) *Six Thinking Hats*. London: Penguin Books.

DfE (Department for Education) (2011) *The Framework for the National Curriculum. A report by the Expert Panel for the National Curriculum review*. London: DfE.

DfES (Department for Education and Skills) (2002) *Time for Standards: Reforming the School Workforce*. London: DfES.

DfES (2003a) *Speaking, Listening, Learning: Working with Children in Key Stages 1 and 2. Teaching Objectives and Classroom Activities*. Norwich: HMSO.

DfES (2003b) *Targetting Support: Choosing and Implementing Interventions for Children with Significant Literacy Difficulties. Management Guidance*. London: DfES.

DfES (2005) *Higher Standards, Better Schools for All*. Norwich: The Stationery Office.

Dixon, A. (1989) Deliver us from eagles, in G. Barrett (ed.) *Disaffection from School*. London: Routledge.

Douglas, J. W. B. (1964) *The Home and the School*. London: MacGibbon and Kee.

Drummond, M. J. (2003) *Assessing Children's Learning*, 2nd ed. London: David Fulton.

Drummond, M. J. (2012) *Assessing Children's Learning*. London: Routledge Classic Edition.

Dweck, C. S. (2000) *Self-Theories: Their Role in Motivation, Personality, and Development*. Philadelphia, PA: Taylor and Francis.

Dweck, C. S. (2008) *Mindset. The New Psychology of Success*. New York: Ballantyne Books.

Dweck, C. S. and Leggett, E. (1988) A social-cognitive approach to motivation and personality, *Psychological Review*, 95: 256–73.

Eisner, E. W. (2004) What can education learn from the arts about the practice of education?, *International Journal of Education and the Arts*, 5(4): 1–12.

Fielding, M. and Moss, P. (2011) *Radical Education and the Common School: A Democratic Alternative*. London: Routledge.

Florian, L. and Linklater, H. (2010) Preparing teachers for inclusive education: using inclusive pedagogy to enhance teaching and learning for all, *Cambridge Journal of Education*, 40(4): 369–86.

Ford, J. (1969) *Social Class and the Comprehensive School*. London: Routledge and Kegan Paul.

Fullan, M. (2003) *The Moral Imperative of School Leadership*. London: Sage Publications.

Gardner, H. (1983) *Frames of Mind: The Theory of Multiple Intelligences*. New York: Basic Books.

General Teaching Council website (2008) Carl Rogers and classroom climate. Accessed 2 July 2011 from www.gtce.org.uk/tla/rft/rogers1008.

Gillborn, D. and Youdell, D. (2000) *Rationing Education: Policy, Practice, Reform and Equity*. Buckingham: Open University Press.

Goldstein, H. and Noss, R. (1990) Against the stream, *FORUM for Promoting 3–19 Comprehensive Education*, 33(1): 4–6.

Good, T. and Brophy, J. (1991) *Looking in Classrooms*, 5th ed. New York: HarperCollins.

Gregory, E. (1993) Sweet and sour: learning to read in a British and Chinese school, *English in Education*, 27: 53–9.

Gregory, E. (1994) Cultural assumptions and early years pedagogy: the effect of the home culture on minority children's interpretation of reading in school, *Language, Culture and Curriculum*, 7: 111–24.

Gregory, E. (1998) Siblings as mediators of literacy in linguistic minority communities, *Language and Education*, 12: 33–54.

Gregory, E. (2000) Recognising differences: reinterpreting family involvement in early literacy, in T. Cox (ed.) *Combating Educational Disadvantage: Meeting the Needs of Vulnerable Children*. London: Falmer.

Gregory, E., Mace, J., Rashid, N. and Williams, A. (1996) *Family Literacy History and Children's Learning Strategies at Home and at School. Final Report of ESRC Project* (No. R000221186).

Hacker, R. G., Rowe, M. J. and Evans, R. D. (1991) The influences of ability groupings for secondary science lessons upon classroom processes. Part 1: Homogeneous groupings (Science Education Notes), *School Science Review*, 73(262): 125–9.

Hargreaves, D. (1967) *Social Relations in a Secondary School*. London: Routledge and Kegan Paul.

Hargreaves, D. (1972) *Interpersonal Relations and Education*. London: Routledge and Kegan Paul.

Hargreaves, D. (1980) Social class, the curriculum and the low achiever, in E. C. Raybould, B. Roberts and K. Wedell (eds) *Helping the Low Achiever in the Secondary School*. Birmingham: University of Birmingham.

Hargreaves, D. (1982) *The Challenge for the Comprehensive School: Culture, Curriculum and Community*. London: Routledge and Kegan Paul.

Harrison, R. ([1963] 1995) Defences and the need to know, in *The Collected Papers of Roger Harrison*. London: McGraw-Hill Book Company.

Hart, S. (1996) *Beyond Special Needs: Enhancing Children's Learning through Innovative Thinking*. London: Paul Chapman Publishing.

Hart, S. (2000) *Thinking through Teaching: A Framework for Enhancing Participation and Learning*. London: David Fulton.

Hart, S., Dixon, A., Drummond, M. J. and McIntyre, D. (2004) *Learning without Limits*. Maidenhead: Open University Press.

Holt, J. (1990) *How Children Fail*, revised ed. Harmondsworth: Penguin Books.

Howe, M. J. A. (1997) *The IQ in Question*. London: Sage Publications.

Hull, R. (1985) *The Language Gap. How Classroom Dialogue Fails*. London: Methuen.

Hymer, B. (2006) Gifted and talented? Time for a re-think?, *Teaching Thinking and Creativity*, 20: 28–31.

Hymer, B. (2009) *Gifted and Talented Pocketbook*. Hampshire: Teachers' Pocketbooks.

Isaacs, S. (1933) *Social Development in Young Children*. London: Routledge and Kegan Paul.

Jackson, B. (1964) *Streaming: An Education System in Miniature*. London: Routledge and Kegan Paul.

Jackson, P. (1968) *Life in Classrooms*. New York: Holt, Rinehart and Winston.

Keddie, N. (1971) Classroom knowledge, in M. F. D. Young (ed.) *Knowledge and Control: New Directions for the Sociology of Education*. London: Collier Macmillan.

Kelly, G. A. (1955) *The Psychology of Personal Constructs*. New York: Norton.

Kettle's Yard (2006) *Lines of Enquiry: Thinking through Drawing*, 15 July–17 September. Accessed 4 June 2011 from http://www.kettlesyard.co.uk/exhibitions/archive/linesofenq.html.

Kincheloe, J., Steinberg, S. R. and Villaverde, L. E. (eds) (1999) *Rethinking Intelligence: Confronting Psychological Assumptions about Teaching and Learning*. London: Routledge.

Kutnick, P., Blatchford, P. and Baines, E. (2002) Pupil grouping in primary school classrooms: sites for learning and social pedagogy? *British Educational Research Journal*, 28: 189–208.

Kutnick, P., Sebba, J., Blatchford, P., Galton, M. and Thorp, J. (2005) *The Effects of Pupil Grouping. Research Report* (No. RR688). London: DfES.

Lacey, C. (1970) *Hightown Grammar: The School as a Social System*. Manchester: Manchester University Press.

Lucas, B. and Claxton, G. (2010) *New Kinds of Smart: How the Science of Learnable Intelligence Is Changing Education*. Maidenhead: Open University Press.

Maddock, M. (2006) Children's personal learning agendas at home, *Cambridge Journal of Education*, 36(2): 153–69.

Moss, P. (2001) Listen in: the importance of consulting with children, *Nursery World*, 5th July: 16–17.

Nash, R. (1973) *Classrooms Observed. The Teacher's Perception and the Pupil's Performance*. London: Routledge and Kegan Paul.

Oakes, J. (1982) The reproduction of inequity: the content of secondary school tracking, *The Urban Review*, 14(2): 107–20.

Oakes, J. (1985) *Keeping Track: How Schools Structure Inequality*. New Haven, CT: Yale University Press.

Peacock, A. (2006) Escaping from the bottom set: finding a voice for school improvement, *Improving Schools*, 9 (3 November): 251–9.

Peacock, A. (2011) Beyond assessment levels: reaching for new heights in primary education, *Education Review,* 23(2): 14–22.

Pearl, A. (1997) Democratic education as an alternative to deficit thinking, in R. Valencia (ed.) *The Evolution of Deficit Thinking: Educational Thought and Practice*. London: Falmer.

Perkins. (1999) *Outsmarting IQ: The Emerging Science of Learnable Intelligence*. New York: The Free Press.

Rist, R. (1971) Student social class and teacher expectations: the self-fulfilling prophecy in ghetto education, *Harvard Educational Review*, 40: 411–51.

Rogers, C. (1969) *Freedom to Learn*. Columbus, OH: Merrill.

Rogers, C. (1983) *Freedom to Learn for the 80s*. Columbus, OH: Merrill.

Rogers, C. and Freiberg, H. J. (1994) *Freedom to Learn*, 3rd ed. New York: Macmillan College Publishing.

Rosenthal, R. and Jacobson, L. (1968) *Pygmalion in the Classroom: Teacher Expectation and Pupils' Intellectual Development*. New York: Holt, Rinehart and Winston.

Salmon, P. (1995) *Psychology in the Classroom: Reconstructing Teachers and Learners*. London: Cassell.

Schon, D. A. (1988) Coaching reflective teaching, in P. P. Grimmett and G. L. Erickson (eds) *Reflection in Teacher Education*. New York: Teachers' College Press.

Simon, B. (1978) Intelligence testing and the comprehensive school, in B. Simon (ed.) *Intelligence, Psychology and Education*. London: Lawrence and Wishart.

Smith, J. K. (2007) How does the development of a shared meta-language impact on children's self-assessment of their own learning? Unpublished MEd thesis. University of Hertfordshire, Hatfield.

Stenhouse, L. (1975) *An Introduction to Curriculum Research and Development*. London: Heinemann.

Stenhouse, L. (1985) *Research as a Basis for Teaching*. London: Heinemann.

Suknandan, L. and Lee, B. (1998) *Streaming, Setting and Grouping by Ability. A Review of the Literature*. Slough: NFER.

Taylor, C. (2009) Learning through a foundation degree. Unpublished PhD thesis. University of Nottingham.

Taylor, N. (1993) Ability grouping and its effect on pupil behaviour: a case study of a Midlands comprehensive school, *Education Today*, 43(2): 14–17.

Tizard, B., Blatchford, P., Burke, J., Farquhar, C. and Plewis, I. (1988) *Young Children at School in the Inner City*. Hove: Lawrence Erlbaum Associates.

Tizard, B. and Hughes, M. (1984) *Young Children Learning*. London: Fontana.

Valencia, R. R. (ed.) (1997) *The Evolution of Deficit Thinking: Educational Thought and Practice*. London: Falmer.

Vandewalle, M. (2010) Come rain or shine: a whole-school approach to forest School, *FORUM for Promoting 3–19 Comprehensive Education*, 52(1): 43–47.

Watson, A. (2001) Low attainers exhibiting higher order mathematical thinking, *Support for Learning*, 16(4): 179–83.

Watson, A. (2006) *Raising Achievement in Secondary Mathematics*. Maidenhead: Open University Press.

Watson, A. (2011) Mathematics and comprehensive ideals, *FORUM for Promoting 3–19 Comprehensive Education*, 53(1): 145–51.

Watson, A. and De Geest, E. (2008) *Changes in Mathematics Teaching Project*. Accessed 31 May 2011 from www.cmp.co.uk.

Watson, A., De Geest, E. and Prestage, S. (2003) *Deep Progress in Mathematics. The Improving Attainment in Mathematics Project*. Oxford: Department for Educational Studies, University of Oxford.

West, T. (1991) *In the Mind's Eye: Visual Thinkers, Gifted People with Learning Difficulties, Computer Images, and the Ironies of Creativity*. New York: Prometheus Books.

White, J. (2005) Howard Gardner: The Myth of Multiple Intelligences. *Viewpoint* 16. London: Institute of Education.

White, J. (2006) *Intelligence, Destiny and Education: The Ideological Roots of Intelligence Testing*. London: Routledge.

Appendix A
How fixed ability thinking can limit learning. Pointers from research

For detailed discussion see Hart *et al.* (2004).

Effects on teachers

- Ability labelling shapes teachers' attitudes towards children and limits their expectations for some children's learning. Teachers vary their teaching and respond differently towards children viewed as 'bright', 'average' or 'less able' (e.g. Jackson 1964; Rosenthal and Jacobson 1968; Keddie 1971; Croll and Moses 1985; Good and Brophy 1991; Hacker, Rowe and Evans 1991; Suknandan and Lee 1998).
- Fixed ability thinking reduces teachers' sense of their own power to promote learning and development through the use of their expertise and professional judgement. It therefore discourages creativity and inventiveness to overcome difficulties (e.g. Kelly 1955; Bloom 1976; Simon 1978; Dixon 1989; Drummond 2003; Hart 1996, 2000).
- Fixed ability thinking encourages teachers to see differential performance as natural and inevitable, and so diverts attention from the part that school and classroom processes play in enabling or limiting learning for individuals and groups (e.g. Jackson 1964; Bernstein 1971; Rist 1971; Coard 1971; Bourdieu 1976; Tizard and Hughes 1984).

Effects on young people

- Young people learn how they are perceived by teachers and respond to that perception; they tend to live up to or down to expectations (e.g. Rosenthal and Jacobson 1968; Nash 1973; Tizard *et al.* 1988; Good and Brophy 1991).

- Ability labelling undermines many young people's dignity, their self-belief, their hopes and expectations for their own learning. It strips them of their sense of themselves as competent, creative human beings, leading them to adopt self-protective strategies that are inimical to learning (e.g. Hargreaves 1967, 1982; Jackson 1968; Lacey 1970; Ball 1981; Holt 1990; Pearl 1997; Dweck 2000).
- Fixed ability thinking and ability-led practices tend to disadvantage some groups of young people. Research has repeatedly drawn attention to social class and ethnicity-based inequalities in the processes of selection, grouping and differentiation of curricula (e.g. Douglas 1964; Jackson 1964; CACE 1967; Ford 1969; Brice Heath 1983; Taylor 1993; Gillborn and Youdell 2000).

Effects on curriculum

- Fixed ability thinking encourages and legitimates a narrow view of curriculum, learning and achievement (e.g. Hargreaves 1980; Alexander 1984, 2001; Goldstein and Noss 1990).
- By naturalizing explanations of differential achievement, fixed-ability thinking perpetuates the limitations and biases built into existing curricula (e.g. Gardner 1983; West 1991).
- Ability labelling and grouping by ability restrict the range of learning opportunities to which individual pupils are exposed (e.g. Jackson 1964; Nash 1973; Oakes 1982, 1985; Hacker et al. 1991; Boaler 1997a, 1997b; Suknandan and Lee 1998; Boaler et al. 2000).
- Ability labelling and grouping encourage schools and teachers to privilege psychometric knowledge of young people over the knowledge acquired through day-to-day classroom interaction (e.g. Kelly 1955; Hull 1985; Hart et al. 2004).

Appendix B
Research approach

Key participants

The headteacher	• Researched her own practice and was a key source of information for the university researchers. She was interviewed, kept a journal for two years and took part in over 30 day-long research meetings.
Individual teachers	• Participation in the research was voluntary. • Six members of teaching staff were interviewed and conducted individual teacher enquiries.
Children	• Three volunteers were sought from each class. Children decided how to select volunteers fairly. Year 6 children devised questions with a researcher, interviewed possible participants, and selected participants based on their responses.
Parents	• Parents of the volunteer children participated in small group interviews. • Transcripts were collected of learning review meetings.

Research questions

The power of collective action	What possibilities for transforming learning capacity come within teachers' remit when a group of staff work together to identify and lift limits on learning, in the interests of the whole student community?
Individual teacher development	What are teachers' experiences of and responses to working within a *Learning without Limits* ethos? • How do the choices teachers make in their pedagogy relate to the school ethos? How do they evolve over time? • What tensions or problems do teachers experience and how do they deal with them? • What support do they need and/or find helpful (from within/without the school setting? From pupils/parents?)

	• Are there key turning points or significant incidents in teachers' thinking and practice over the lifetime of the project? • How do teachers' choices, the problems they encounter and their solutions to these problems confirm, modify or extend our initial model of *Learning without Limits* pedagogy?
School leadership	What issues face school leaders who want to develop schools committed to learning without limits? • How do they successfully manage the tensions and conflicts between their own development agenda and the requirements of national policy? • How do they communicate their purposes and values to, and win the support of, other bodies, for example parents and governors? • What support needs to be provided for classroom teachers? Does the model of pedagogy derived from previous research also apply to this task? • How can pupils themselves be enabled to work on a whole-school basis as active agents in the development of their own and each other's learning capacities?
The role of parents/ communities	What part do parents play, positively or negatively, in supporting or limiting the influence that teachers and schools can have in trans-forming learning capacity? • How do parents come to understand what the school stands for and how the school works? • How can schools actively promote the positive contribution that parents/communities can make? • How can the headteacher/members of the leadership team best communicate the central ideas of *Learning without Limits* to the community of parents/governors (etc.)?

Phase 1

Open-ended interviews with the headteacher (HT)	• Established base line of the history of the school's develop-ment since her arrival in 2003. • Elicited vision for the future related to the values and ethos to be created in the school. • Captured key events and issues as they arose in school. • HT's plans and questions provided framework for observing and documenting what was happening in and around the school. • Documented HT perceptions of opportunities, needs, steps that she could take to support teachers, other school staff, pupils and parents.

Open-ended interviews with teachers	• Key formative influences and experiences in the development of thinking about teaching and learning identified. • Baseline of teacher thinking and classroom practices at the beginning of the research period established. • Investigated and documented in-depth issues, dilemmas, possibilities and constraints. • Key constructs, areas of concern and arising questions for each teacher identified. • How HT's aspirations and initiatives were experienced and responded to. • Factors which facilitated or constrained development. • Recorded relevant aspects of existing school and classroom practices, aspirations, actions taken. • Collected teachers' own accounts of what they were trying to do and to achieve which provided the frameworks for the study of what happened in their classrooms.
Headteacher (HT) journal	• Recorded day-to-day actions, decisions, key areas of concern, significant events around school, for herself and her colleagues.
Children	• Collected children's views of their experience of learning in the school and the choices they are able to make.
Whole-staff meeting at Wroxham	• University researchers explained the rationale for the individual teacher enquiries, teachers discussed areas of current thinking and practice they wished to explore in depth.

Phase 2

Focus	• Explored in depth an aspect of each teacher's practice. • Pressing concerns and questions teachers identified in Phase 1 formed the focus of the individual teacher enquiries based on the practices they intended to develop or introduce in their classrooms. • Explored the teachers' experiences, developing thinking and practice. • Documented teachers' learning from their classroom enquiries. • Documented the children's experiences in the classrooms. • Supported planning research methods to tighten initial ideas, develop research questions and plan data collection.
Participant observation and semi-structured interviews with teachers	• Classroom observations, immediately followed by open-ended reflective interview. • Observation field notes shared with each teacher, followed by semi-structured interview.

	• Individual and/or group interviews with children as part of teachers' data collection. • Emerging understandings shared with each teacher, reflection on the experience and evidence, new questions identified, refined plans for the second cycle of teachers' individual enquiries. • Provided support with planning research methods for next cycle of investigation. • Second cycle of classroom observations, immediately followed by open-ended reflective interview. Observation field notes shared with each teacher, followed by semi-structured interview.
HT interviews and journal	• Established the role taken in supporting, extending or driving teachers' individual enquiries. • Continued to explore vision, values and ethos. • Captured further key events and issues as they arose in school. • Documented HT's aspirations, any initiatives, perception of opportunities, needs and support offered to teachers. • Continued to record day-to-day actions, decisions, key areas of concern, significant events around school, for herself and her colleagues in the journal.
Interviews with children	• Children's views of their experience of learning in the school and the choices they are able to make.
Group interviews with parents of the focus children	• Views on aspects of the school's work that were salient for them. • Their beliefs about their own children's current and future learning capacities.

Phase 3

Formal analysis and writing up	• In-depth analysis of all data. • Critical incident charting interviews with each teacher. • Accounts of each teacher's thinking and practice during the research period developed and shared with each teacher and validated by them. • Searching across the accounts for common themes and differences. • Sustained dialogue with the HT during research meetings. • Draft writing shared with the school staff so that they were able to read and comment on our interpretations of the data in the writing-up stage.

Appendix C
Rethinking notions of IQ and 'intelligence'

Some useful readings

Balchin, Hymer and Matthews (2009) *The Routledge International Companion to Gifted Education*. **London: Routledge**

One of the co-editors of this book, Barry Hymer, who has for many years been a consultant in 'gifted education', challenges assumptions about 'ability' and 'giftedness' associated with national policy around 'gifted education'. His alternative, inclusive conceptualization (enhancing quality of provision for all, rather than identification of individuals for special treatment), is echoed by many contributors to the book.

Bloom (1976) *Human Characteristics and School Learning*. **New York: McGraw-Hill**

Bloom argues that, under the right conditions, most students could achieve in school at a level previously thought to be attainable only by a small minority. Wide variations in students' attainments can be understood in terms of alterable factors: the skills required for the task, the motivation to carry out the task and quality of instruction, including attention to success of each student's learning. His 'mastery learning' model of pedagogy focuses on what teachers can do to create the conditions that reduce variation and optimize all students' opportunities for effective learning.

Bruner (1996) *The Culture of Education*. **Cambridge, MA: Harvard University Press**

In this book, Bruner criticizes his own earlier work for being overly concerned with 'solo, intra-psychic processes', what goes on 'inside the head'. He develops his new thesis that 'culture shapes the mind, providing us with the toolkit with which we construct . . . our worlds'. He argues that schools must 'constantly re-assess what school does to the young student's concept of his own powers'.

Chitty (2009)   *Eugenics, Race, Intelligence and Education*. **London: Continuum**
This fascinating, scholarly study examines how 'a belief in genetic
determinism in the area of human intellectual capacity grew out of a set
of ideas about sustaining and improving the quality of the human race,
and then went on to profoundly influence the structure of the British
education system'. In the final chapter, 'Prospects for the future', Chitty
draws extensively on arguments and evidence in *Learning without Limits*
to explore the scope for building an education system based on belief in
the fundamental educability of all young people.

Claxton (1990)   *Teaching to Learn: A Direction for Education*. **London: Cassell**
Claxton elaborates a theory of learning that 'casts doubt on the validity
and even the existence of the construct of ability'. He suggests that
learners possess a whole repertoire of learning strategies, some of which
are relevant to school but not available, some of which are available and
not relevant, and some of which are both available and relevant. The
repertoire is learnable and can be developed. 'If people's learning power
does not develop, this is due not to a "lack of ability" but to the absence
of appropriate experiences, and/or of the emotional or situational
conditions which enable those people to explore and extend the current
boundaries of their skills as learners' (pp. 35–6).

Dweck (2000)   *Self-Theories: Their Role in Motivation, Personality and
Development*. **Philadelphia, PA: Taylor and Francis**
Dweck's research explores how young people's views of ability impact on
their attitudes and learning. She distinguishes between an 'entity' and an
'incremental' theory of ability. People who hold an entity view interpret
success or failure in learning as being due to a mysterious entity inside the
learner that is fixed, so he or she can do nothing about it; people who hold
an incremental view of ability, on the other hand, believe that their ability
can grow and develop. They respond to difficulty or failure by reflecting
on their strategies and finding out what they need to do or learn in order
to be successful next time. Dweck also looks at what educators can do (for
example through styles of feedback) to foster an incremental view of
ability in their learners, and how it affects learning outcomes when there is
a shift of mindset from an entity theory to an incremental theory of ability.

Gardner (1983) *Frames of Mind: The Theory of Multiple Intelligences*. **New York:
Basic Books**
Gardner argues that traditional views of intelligence are far too narrow to
encompass the full range of what we understand as intelligent behaviour.
In addition to the logico-mathematical and linguistic intelligence focused
on in IQ tests (and favoured in school curricula and examinations), he
identifies other kinds of intelligence: musical, spatial, bodily-kinaesthetic,
interpersonal and intra-personal. To qualify for inclusion in the list, an
'intelligence' must demonstrate problem-solving and problem-creating
skills that are important within a cultural context.

Howe (1997)	***The IQ in Question*. London: Sage Publications** Howe argues that 'the received wisdom on human intelligence rests on unsound assumptions, faulty reasoning and inadequate evidence'. Intelligence is real enough, he says, but only in the sense that success and happiness are real. It is an outcome . . . but it is not a cause. This very accessible and readable book elaborates the basis for Howe's critique and develops more complex explanations for perceived differences of 'intelligence'. It challenges claims about the racial origins of IQ differences, the apparently restricted changeability of intelligence, the assumption that intelligence is measurable in the way that physical qualities are measurable, and the use of IQ scores to predict high individual achievements.
Hymer (2006)	**Gifted and Talented? Time for a re-think?** *Teaching Thinking and Creativity*, **Issue 20** See also http://www.teachingexpertise.com/articles/gifted-talented-timerethink-119. Hymer explains his concerns about current policies relating to 'Gifted and Talented' education, and especially with regard to the concept itself which he regards as 'deeply problematic'. He draws on the work of Carol Dweck (see above) to argue that '21st century evidence suggests that we can change not only students' intelligence, but also their beliefs about their intelligence'. Unfortunately, he says, it is the fixed, entity view of intelligence that informs current national policies in this area. The eschewal of fuzzy concepts like ability altogether is 'the truly radical option', he continues (citing *Learning without Limits*) as an example of how this can be realized in practice). Meanwhile, educators need to be open to radical reformulations of what we mean by intelligence and achievement, and to non-normative, non-deterministic concepts of gifts and talents.
Hymer (2009)	***Gifted and Talented Pocketbook*. Alresford, Hampshire: Teachers' Pocketbooks** In this book, Hymer explains and develops his alternative, inclusive approach to 'a gifted education where all pupils are stretched, challenged and engaged'. The book sets out the theoretical ideas in a very readable and accessible way, and includes a detailed exploration of practical approaches reflecting the ideas.
Kincheloe, Steinberg and Villaverde (eds) (1999)	***Rethinking Intelligence: Confronting Psychological Assumptions about Teaching and Learning*. London: Routledge** A collection of articles intended to challenge traditional views of intelligence (as fixed and innate, with only a privileged few being endowed with superior intelligence), elaborate alternative constructions and consider the implications for practice. 'When we challenge these perspectives, dramatic changes occur in our perceptions of who is capable of learning. Such a challenge moves educators to take a giant first step in the effort to make schooling a democratic enterprise' (p. 8). Argues the need for teachers to be better equipped to study and make sense of the social context within which their students are situated. 'They must become researchers of their students, understanding the way

learners' backgrounds mesh and conflict with the culture of schools . . . In this way teachers come to understand themselves . . . and their relationship to the contexts of those they teach' (p. 12).

| **Lucas and Claxton (2010)** | ***New Kinds of Smart: How the Science of Learnable Intelligence is Changing Education.* Maidenhead: Open University Press** |

Lucas and Claxton argue that scientific developments relating to the understanding of intelligence have yet to be incorporated into the education system. Many myths about intelligence (including the idea that it is fixed) continue to influence policy and practice. They review recent research and thinking on the nature of intelligence and explore how these new ways of thinking can (and are beginning to) open up hitherto unexplored possibilities for education.

| **Perkins (1999)** | ***Outsmarting IQ: The Emerging Science of Learnable Intelligence.* New York: The Free Press** |

Perkins identifies different dimensions of intelligence: neural, experiential and reflective. He argues that experiential and reflective intelligence can both be advanced by learning – 'experiential intelligence through in depth experiences and reflective intelligence through the cultivation of strategies, attitudes and metacognition'. His concept of 'distributed intelligence' links to the *Learning without Limits* idea of learning capacity having a 'collective' as well as an individual dimension. Perkins contrasts the 'person-solo' ('the dance of the naked brain') with the 'person-plus', i.e. intelligent behaviour that occurs in a supportive physical, social and cultural context. 'The inward look leads us only to think of training minds of various kinds in various ways. The outward look of distributed intelligence tells us to pay heed to the physical, social and symbolic setting' (p. 323).

| **Simon (1978)** | `**Intelligence testing and the comprehensive school', in B. Simon (ed.)** *Intelligence, Psychology and Education.* **London: Lawrence and Wishart** |

Simon presents a detailed critique of intelligence testing, identifying the logical, statistical and philosophical problems associated with it. In the absence of an agreed understanding of intelligence and means of measuring intelligence *per se*, psychometricians focused on measuring differences between students in the performance of particular 'mental' tasks. This has left as a legacy the assumption that it is important, in education generally, to focus on differences between children. Simon concludes that 'it is difficult to contemplate with patience a practice which may determine a child's whole future at age 7, which inculcates a sense of failure and inadequacy among a substantial proportion of our young citizens, a sense of failure constantly reinforced and extraordinarily difficult to overcome'.

| **Valencia (ed.) (1997)** | ***The Evolution of Deficit Thinking: Educational Thought and Practice.* London: Falmer** |

Especially chapter by Arthur Pearl, 'Democratic education as an alternative to deficit thinking'.

'Deficit thinking' refers to the idea that internal deficits in students and their families are the reason that students (particularly those of low-income, racial/ethnic minority background) fail in school. The presumed 'deficits' include limited intelligence, alongside lack of motivation and limited family support. This collection of essays explores and critiques genetic, cultural and family variants of deficit thinking and offers alternative explanations of why students fail. On the *Learning without Limits* team, we were particularly interested in Arthur Pearl's chapter in which he develops his theory of democratic education as an alternative to deficit thinking. Pearl explains how 'unequal encouragements' contribute to lasting social inequity, the enduring hierarchy of privilege and wealth and the important inequalities that are created and maintained in classrooms. The alternative is to recognize the desires that are universal to all human beings, and to reconstruct classrooms so that these desires are equally fulfilled for all students.

White (2005)   **Howard Gardner: The Myth of Multiple Intelligences.** *Viewpoint* **(16). London: Institute of Education**
White provides a detailed critique of Gardner's theory of multiple intelligences (see above), focusing particularly on Chapter 4, 'What is intelligence?'. He identifies many flaws in the selection and justification of the seven intelligences (later extended to nine) and in the developmentalist theory that underpins the whole project. He concludes that the theory is 'flaky' and (despite having some positive impact on curricula, teaching methods and expectations of students) can also potentially be used to encourage divisive educational policies and determinist beliefs about differential, inborn ceilings of potential in relation to the different intelligences.

White (2006)   *Intelligence, Destiny and Education: The Ideological Roots of Intelligence Testing.* **London: Routledge**
This book explores the origins of traditional views of intelligence and their links with the subject-based school curriculum. Arguing that there are no solid grounds for innate differences in IQ or for the traditional subject-based curriculum, White traces both back to the protestant Reformation of the 16th century, and specifically to the more radical forms of protestantism which formed the puritan and dissenting communities of the 17th century and afterwards on both sides of the Atlantic. 'We need to become aware of these roots of our conventional perspectives,' White argues, 'so that we can, where appropriate, make ourselves free of them.' He concludes by arguing for a school curriculum based around notions of personal fulfilment, formulated in a way that makes personal flourishing available to everyone rather than being reserved for a deserving minority.

Index

LEARNING WITHOUT LIMITS

Susan Hart, Annabelle Dixon,
Mary Jane Drummond & Donald McIntyre

978-0-335-21259-0 (Paperback)
March 2004

eBook also available

This book explores ways of teaching that are free from determinist beliefs about ability. In a detailed critique of the practices of ability labelling and ability-focussed teaching, *Learning without Limits* examines the damage these practices can do to young people, teachers and the curriculum.

Drawing on a research project at the University of Cambridge, the book features nine vivid case studies (from Year 1 to Year 11) that describe how teachers have developed alternative practices despite considerable pressure on them and on their schools and classrooms.

www.openup.co.uk

 **OPEN UNIVERSITY PRESS**
McGraw - Hill Education

NEW KINDS OF SMART
How the Science of Learnable
Intelligence is Changing Education

Bill Lucas and Guy Claxton

9780335236183 (Paperback)
2010

20th Century schools presumed that students' intelligence was largely fixed. 21st century science says that intelligence is expandable - and in a variety of ways. *New Kinds of Smart* argues that this shift in the way we think about young minds opens up hitherto unexplored possibilities for education.

Each chapter presents:

- Practical examples
- Tools and templates so that each new strand of thinking can be woven into your work as teachers and into your lives as learners

www.openup.co.uk    OPEN UNIVERSITY PRESS
                                        McGraw - Hill Education

DEVELOPING REFLECTIVE PRACTICE
A Guide for Beginning Teachers

Deb McGregor & Lesley Cartwright

978-0-33524-257-3 (Paperback)
September 2011

eBook also available

This student friendly practical guide helps you get to grips with reflective practice in teaching, through bite-sized sections that are informative and quickly digestible. The book clearly explains some of the best-known theories on reflective practice and then shows how reflection on and in practice can have a positive impact on classroom performance.

The book includes illustrative case studies considering how reflective practice can inform your teaching practice, including:

- Preparing for teaching
- Fitting into your school
- Designing lessons
- Managing behavior
- Planning for creativity
- Assessing effectively
- Developing essential teaching techniques
- Working effectively with your mentor
- Extending your professional practice at Master's level

www.openup.co.uk